# MAKING MEMORIES

MONTH BY MONTH

Poems, Art Projects, & Activity Ideas
for Creating Student Scrapbooks

## Written by
Kathy Wootton

**Editor:** Carla Hamaguchi
**Illustrator:** Darcy Tom
**Cover Photographer:** Michael Jarrett
**Cover Illustrator:** Kimberlee Graves
**Designer:** Corina Chien
**Cover Designer:** Corina Chien
**Art Director:** Tom Cochrane
**Project Director:** Carolea Williams

# TABLE OF CONTENTS

Introduction ..................................................................3

## Everything You Need to Know

Using This Book ..........................................................4
Parent Involvement......................................................6
Choosing a Format ......................................................8
Organization and Storage ..........................................9
Basic Scrapbooking Techniques................................10
Creative Options .......................................................11
Putting It All Together.................................................12

## Monthly Ideas and Layouts

September ...............................................................13
October....................................................................23
November...............................................................34
December................................................................46
January....................................................................58
February...................................................................70
March......................................................................82
April .......................................................................93
May.......................................................................103
June.......................................................................113
July/August............................................................125

## Additional Scrapbook Resources

Our Field Trip..........................................................136
Month Headlines .....................................................137
Captions .................................................................140
Everyone Has Gifts/Parent Letter .............................141
All About Me ..........................................................142
Line Templates........................................................143

# INTRODUCTION

A scrapbook full of art projects that a student makes during the school year is a perfect end-of-the-year gift and keepsake for any child. Add a child's writing samples, math activities, photographs, and projects, and that same memory book becomes a valuable tool for tracking his or her academic progress and communicating it to his or her parents. Whether you are interested in making scrapbooks with your students for fun or for evaluation, the clever ideas and adorable reproducible patterns featured in *Making Memories Month by Month* can make this year-long project easy and exciting.

The memory book described in this resource can be as elaborate or as simple as you wish. You will find several different ways to creatively organize children's work to create unique scrapbooks that also serve as colorful assessment portfolios. No matter how much time or energy you choose to invest in this endeavor, you and your students can have fun working together to create an authentic memento of their academic development over the course of the year.

Examine the activities, poems, writing templates, writing paper, and other resources included in *Making Memories Month by Month*, and choose those that best fit your plan for your scrapbooks. Throughout the school year, collect children's work, take photos, and file them away until you are ready to assemble the scrapbooks. Assembling the books requires minimal supplies. Simply get out your scissors and glue sticks to crop and paste work samples and photos on scrapbook pages. These memorable keepsakes will be cherished by parents and students for years to come.

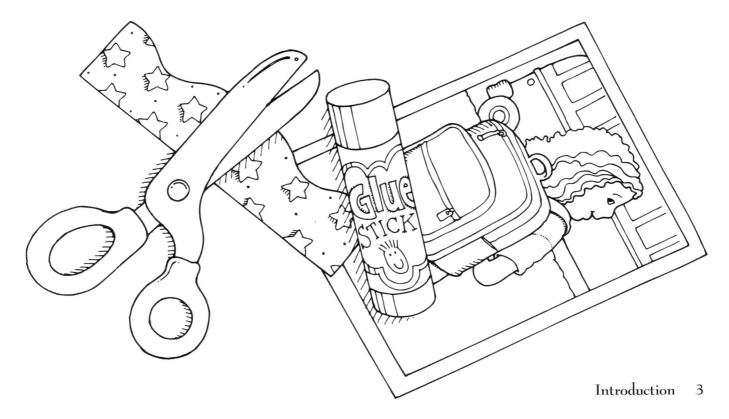

# USING THIS BOOK

This resource contains a year's worth of literature links, activities, poems, and reproducible pages. There are eleven sections, one for each month from September through June and one for July/August. Each section features the following components:

## Sample Layout

The first page of each section features a sample scrapbook page for that month. The sample layout highlights the activities, poems, art projects, and writing template from this book. Use the suggested thematic, seasonal, and holiday ideas to plan additional units of study that complement the book's resources.

## Literature Links

Choose a book from the extensive list to introduce and reinforce each month's activities.

## Activity Ideas

Each activity idea is designed to have children create a piece of artwork or a work sample that corresponds with that month's theme, season, or holiday.

## Handprint Ideas

Each handprint idea coordinates with a song about that month's theme, season, and/or holiday. Follow the detailed directions for painting children's hands. Invite children to make their handprint on a piece of paper, or cover the directions on the handprint idea page with a piece of paper, and copy a class set of the page for children to use for their print. This option allows you to combine that month's song and handprint on the same page. Place these pages in the scrapbooks, or create a

book for each child that includes his or her handprint for each month and title it *My Handprint Book*.

## Poems and Songs

Some activities and art projects incorporate the poems and/or songs for that month. Here are just a few of the many other ways you can use the poems and songs with your class:

✮ Write a poem or song on chart paper, and display it. Invite the class to recite the words. Encourage volunteers to use pointers to point to the words as the class reads.

✮ Write a poem or song on an 8½" x 11" (21.5 cm x 28 cm) piece of paper, and make two copies of it. Glue one copy to the front of a manila envelope. Laminate the other copy, and cut it into word strips. Place the strips in the envelope, and store it at a center. Invite children to put the word strips in order.

## Writing Template

Each month, have children complete the sentence frame or story starter on the reproducible writing template. Allow children who cannot complete the writing on their own to dictate their words. Use a yellow marker to write their words, and have children trace over the letters. Then, invite children to illustrate their writing. Have children write their name on the back of their paper.

## Decorative Writing Paper

Choose a new theme each month for children to write about. For each child, copy the decorative writing paper for that month and copy one of the line templates from pages 143–144. Use the ruled-line template for younger students who need guidance in forming their letters, or use the line template for older students. Show children how to place the line template under their writing paper and then write

about the topic. Ask children to write their name on the back of their paper.

## Monthly Frames

Choose from two frame designs each month. Give each child a frame. Have children use crayons or markers to color their frame. Invite children to cut along the outer edge of their frame and tape or glue a photo to the center of the frame. Or, have children also cut out the interior of the frame to create a "window" and place their photo behind the frame. Have children use the frames to write about special events, class trips, or activities. Use children's completed frames to label photos and/or work samples in their memory books.

# PARENT INVOLVEMENT

Here are some ways to get parents involved and make the scrapbooking process even easier.

## Film Contributions

Send home a letter (page 7) or ask parents at Back-to-School Night to donate film. Or, consider adding a roll of film to the list of school supplies you require your students to bring on the first day of school.

## Copies

Ask parent volunteers to photocopy all of the poetry and/or songs, month headlines, frames, writing templates, and writing paper for the year. Make a file folder for each month, and fill each folder with the corresponding materials.

## Premade Blank Books

Rather than assemble children's scrapbooks at the end of the school year, consider asking parent volunteers to create a blank book for each child at the beginning of the school year. Give volunteers the supplies and directions needed to assemble the blank books. For example, give parent volunteers the materials to make blank books consisting of 12 construction paper pages bound together with yarn. Now, you can assemble the pages as the year progresses.

## Taking Photos

Invite parent volunteers to attend field trips and special class events. Ask one parent to be the designated photographer. Give the parent a disposable camera or roll of film to use in his or her own camera. After a field trip, have each child complete the Our Field Trip reproducible (page 136). Place the completed reproducibles and photos in the scrapbooks.

Dear Parents,

This is a very special year for your child. He or she will be taking part in many activities and learning lots of new concepts. I like to keep track of some of the children's endeavors by taking photos of them while they are working and playing. You know what they say . . . a picture is worth a thousand words.

As you can imagine, plenty of film is required to take all these wonderful photographs. If you are able to donate a roll of film to our class, we would greatly appreciate it!

Thank you,

# CHOOSING A FORMAT

Decide what materials you want to include in the memory books. Then select a format that accommodates these items. Here are some sample page ideas to help you choose the page size and content of your memory books.

**8½" x 12" (21.5 cm x 30.5 cm)**
Include a writing sample, a month headline, and a holiday/seasonal poem or song.

**18" x 12" (46 cm x 30.5 cm)**
Include photos, work samples, a holiday/seasonal poem, and a month headline.

**Two 18" x 12" (46 cm x 30.5 cm) pages**
Include photos, work samples, completed writing templates, clip art, a holiday/seasonal poem or song, and a month headline.

# ORGANIZATION AND STORAGE

There are several ways to organize and store the memory book materials. Here are a few suggestions to get you started.

## File System

Label a separate file folder for each child. As you develop film throughout the year, place each child's picture in his or her individual file folder. Also file samples of children's work you would like to include in their scrapbook. When you are ready to assemble the scrapbooks, you will have what you need all in one place. Try to assemble the pages for each month as you go along. Older children can be a great help by putting their own pages together. Keep children's completed pages in a large covered plastic tub. File the pages in order by month for each child. Then, at the end of the school year, you will only need to make the cover and ending pages.

## Premade Blank Books

Another option is to make a blank book for each child before the school year begins. Decide on the number of pages you want for each month and assemble books accordingly. For example, if you want a cover, two pages for each month, a page for autographs, and a back cover, you would attach 13 sheets of construction paper together. (Items would be glued to the front and back of each construction paper.) Throughout the year, glue the photos and work samples directly on the pages of the children's books.

## Ready-made Pages on Display

You could choose to create a class set of pages each month and use them in a display. Glue each child's work sample on a separate sheet of construction paper. Then, glue a month headline, a holiday/seasonal poem or song, or another decorative piece on the paper to make a page for each child. Display the children's pages on a bulletin board. Take down these ready-made scrapbook pages at the end of the month, and file them away. Repeat the process each month to create fun bulletin board displays and an easy way to organize and assemble your memory books.

# BASIC SCRAPBOOKING TECHNIQUES

There are basic scrapbooking techniques to use to enhance the look of the scrapbooks. Choose one technique, or use them all to create your scrapbook pages.

## Taking Photos

Each month, take a "theme" picture of each child. Also take pictures of the children at work and play. Be sure to take pictures of special events such as the school jog-a-thon, Grandparent's Day, and class field trips. Make sure to get double prints if more than one child is in a picture. That way you can use the same photo in two different scrapbooks. The number of pictures you take is a personal decision. Another option is to have children draw pictures of themselves.

## Cropping Photos

Identify the focal point of each photo, and cut around it. Throw away the unwanted parts. However, in some cases you may want to keep background images (e.g., a museum that you went to on a field trip). When there is more than one child in a photo, you can crop and cut the photo to create two separate photos and place one in each child's scrapbook.

## Matting

Glue the cropped photo or the child's work sample to a piece of colored paper. Trim the paper close to the edges of the photo or work sample. This creates a border or mat that frames the photo or work sample and adds color to the page.

## Cutting Shapes

Cut colored paper into various shapes, and place them behind or overlapping photos or student work samples.

## Using Titles and Captions

Make copies of the month headlines on pages 137–139, and cut them apart. Use the headlines to label the first page of each month in the scrapbooks. Make copies of the captions (page 140), and cut them apart. Glue appropriate captions near photos or work samples.

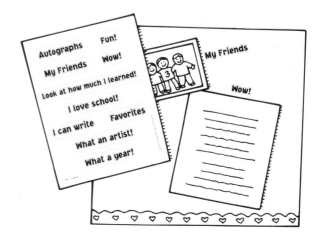

# CREATIVE OPTIONS

There are several types of tools and materials you can use to enhance your scrapbook pages. Here are just a few:

SPECIAL MEMORIES

border tape

patterned paper

paper punch-outs

CTP Show-It-Offs

Red Ribbon
WEEK

CTP Snapshots

CTP Cut-Outs

rubber stamps

ABCDE
FGHIJ
KLMNO
PQRST
UVWXY
Z

stickers

patterned-edged scissors

ribbon

fabric

stencils

# PUTTING IT ALL TOGETHER

## The Cover and Extra Pages

Take a close-up picture of each child for the cover of his or her book. Mount the picture on a background paper (e.g., school-theme stationery, colored paper, or CTP Snapshots), and type the child's name, the year, and the school name on the paper. Mount the completed paper on the cover page of the scrapbook. Copy the Everyone Has Gifts poem/parent letter on page 141, and cut them apart. Glue one or both to the inside of the cover. Laminate the cover.

Write a letter to each child. Tell children how much you enjoyed having them in your class or thank them for being a wonderful student. Attach the letter to the last page of the book. Include a photo of the child and yourself on this page. Laminate the page, and use it as the book's back cover.

Create a page for children to use for their friends' autographs. Make copies of the *Autographs* caption (see page 140), cut it out, and glue it to a blank page in each child's book. Invite children to autograph their classmates' books.

## Binding the Book

Use a plastic binding machine and plastic spiral combs to bind the pages of the books. If you do not have access to a binding machine, punch holes in the pages and connect them with ribbon, yarn, brass fasteners, or metal rings.

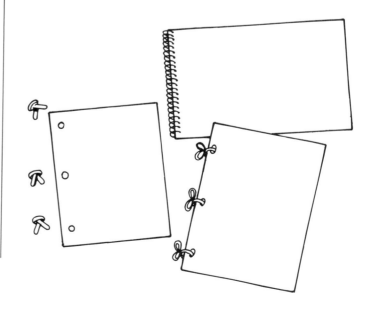

# SEPTEMBER..........................

September is a time to start school, make new friends, work on skills, and learn new information. Activities that boost self-esteem are great for this time of the year. Take pictures of each child, and/or have him or her draw a self-portrait. Label the pictures, and display them around the room to help the class become familiar with one another. Learn more about the children by having them complete an All About Me reproducible (page 142). Place the completed reproducible on a September page in the memory book. September is also a fun time for children to learn about apples.

## Literature Links ...................................

- ☆ *An Apple a Day* by Melvin Berger (Doubleday Books)

- ☆ *Miss Bindergarten Gets Ready for Kindergarten* by Joseph Slate (Dutton)

- ☆ *The Other Emily* by Gibbs Davis (Houghton Mifflin)

- ☆ *Picking Apples and Pumpkins* by Amy & Richard Hutchings (Econo-Clad Books)

- ☆ *Ten Apples Up on Top* by Theodore LeSieg (Random House)

- ☆ *What Will Mommy Do When I'm at School?* by Dolores Johnson (Aladdin)

## Self-Portrait

Trace a circle on a piece of paper for each child. Invite children to create their first self-portrait. Have them draw their face in the circle and then draw a body below the circle. Have children write their name to complete the sentence *I am _____*.

### Materials
- ❏ circle pattern
- ❏ drawing paper
- ❏ crayons or markers

## I'm a Star

Copy a class set of the I'm a Star! reproducible on colored construction paper. Have children draw a self-portrait in the star. Invite children to write or dictate what they think is special about them in the space provided above the star. Encourage children to decorate their star with glue and glitter. Display the children's work on a bulletin board titled *Shining Stars*.

### Materials
- ❏ I'm a Star! reproducible (page 16)
- ❏ construction paper (assorted colors)
- ❏ crayons or markers
- ❏ glue
- ❏ glitter

## Ten Apples Up on Top

### Materials

- *Ten Apples Up on Top* by Theodore LeSieg
- Ten Apples Up on Top reproducible (page 17)
- crayons or markers
- apple stickers or red, green, and yellow crayons
- camera/film
- apple

Read aloud *Ten Apples Up on Top*. Give each child a Ten Apples Up on Top reproducible. Have children add a face, hair, and clothes to the figure. Give each child ten apple stickers, or have children use red, green, and yellow crayons. Have children place or draw ten apples in a pattern on top of their person. Encourage children to tell you what their pattern is (e.g., *My pattern is red, green, yellow, red, green, yellow*). Write each child's response to complete the sentence *Ten apples up on top. My pattern is _____*. Take a photo of each child with an apple on his or her head.

## Paper Plate Apple

### Materials

- small paper plates
- red, green, and yellow paint/ paintbrushes
- scissors
- brown and green scrap paper
- glue
- black beans

Give each child a small paper plate. Invite children to paint their plate red, green, or yellow. Have children cut brown and green scrap paper to make a stem and leaves and glue them to their painted plate to make an apple. Give each child one to ten black beans (seeds) to glue on the back of their plate. Have children find a partner and add together the number of seeds from both plates. Or, say a math problem (e.g., *4 + 1 = ?*), and have children with that number of seeds (e.g., 5) stand.

Children practiced counting while gluing seeds to their "apples."

# I'm a Star!

Nobody can _____

like _____ .

# Ten Apples Up on Top

Ten apples up on top. My pattern is _____, _____,

_____, _____, _____, _____, _____,

_____, _____, _____.

# September

(to the tune of "Are You Sleeping?")

It's September.
It's September.
Fall is near.
Fall is near.
We are making new friends.
We are making new friends.
School is here.
School is here.

## Apple

Paint the palm of each child's hand with red paint. Do not put any paint on children's fingers. Ask them to press their hand on a white piece of paper. Have them dip the pad of their thumb in green paint and press their thumb above the apple print to make a leaf and a stem.

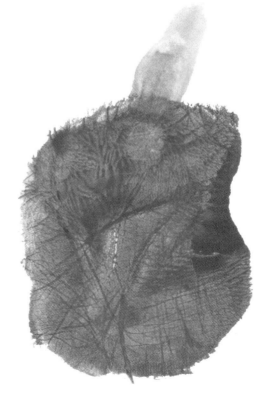

Making Memories Month by Month © 2001 Creative Teaching Press

## Back to School
### (to the tune of "Twinkle, Twinkle, Little Star")

It's September. Fall is here.
It's my favorite time of year.
Boys and girls can make new friends.
Teachers lend a helping hand.
Lots to learn and so much fun.
Back to school for everyone!

## Way Up High

Way up high in an apple tree,
Two little apples smiled at me.
I shook that tree as hard as I could,
And down came the apples,
Mmmm . . . they were good!

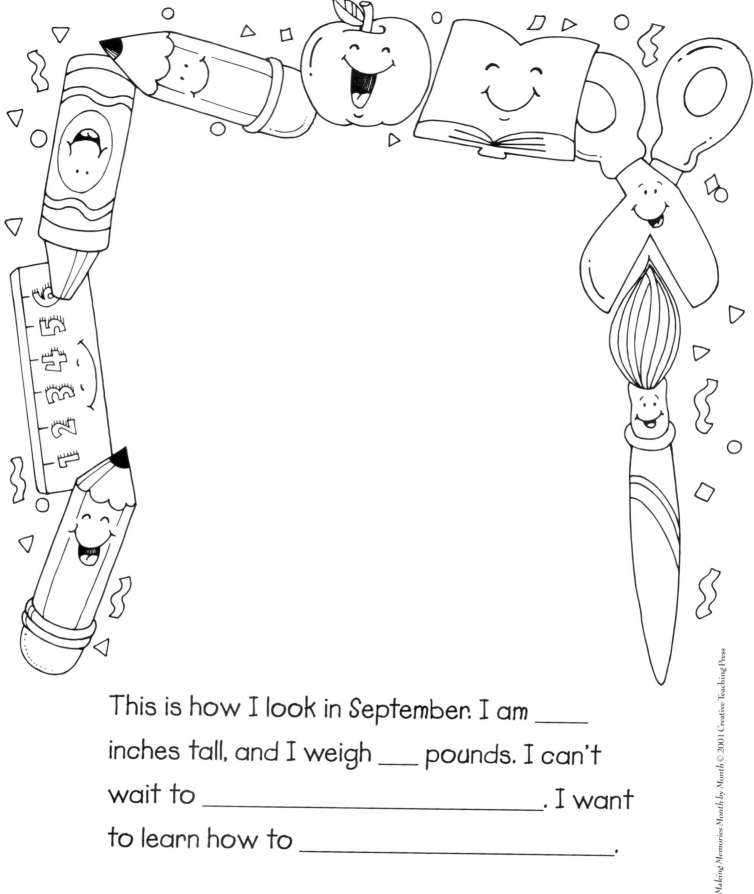

This is how I look in September. I am ____ inches tall, and I weigh ___ pounds. I can't wait to _____. I want to learn how to _____.

Making Memories Month by Month © 2001 Creative Teaching Press

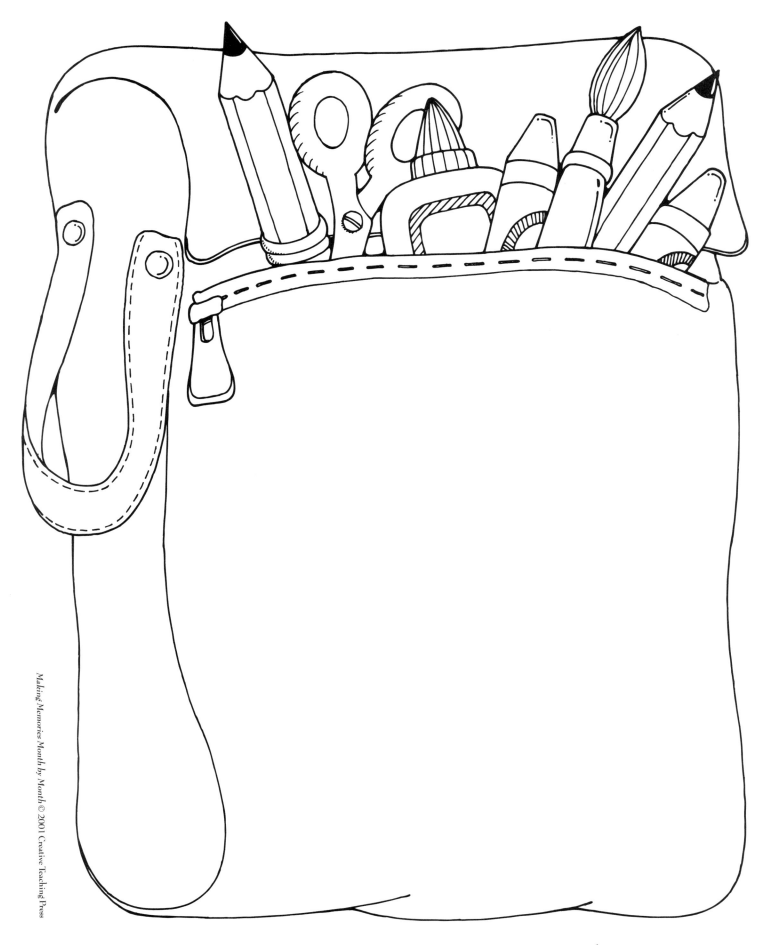

# OCTOBER

October is a wonderful time to teach about fall, fall leaves, harvest time, bats, spiders, pumpkins, scarecrows, and Halloween. If children are allowed to wear their Halloween costumes to school, take individual pictures of them all dressed up. Try to plan a visit to a local pumpkin patch.

## Literature Links

☆ *Autumn Leaves* by Ken Robbins (Scholastic)

☆ *The Biggest Pumpkin Ever* by Steven Kroll (Holiday House)

☆ *The Little Old Lady Who Was Not Afraid of Anything* by Linda Williams (HarperTrophy)

☆ *Pumpkin, Pumpkin* by Jeanne Titherington (William Morrow & Company)

☆ *Red Leaf, Yellow Leaf* by Lois Ehlert (Harcourt)

☆ *The Very Busy Spider* by Eric Carle (Philomel)

## Jack-o'-Lantern

Make a class set of the Pumpkin reproducible on brown construction paper and a class set of the poem "Pumpkin, Pumpkin." Give each child a reproducible, and have children cut out the pumpkin. Have children use orange and yellow scrap paper to create a "tear art" jack-o'-lantern. Show children how to tear the paper and glue it on their pumpkin. Encourage them to overlap their paper pieces. Give each child a copy of the poem, and have children glue it to their pumpkin. Have the class recite the poem together.

Pumpkin, Pumpkin
Pumpkin, pumpkin
Round and fat
Turn into a jack-o'-lantern
Just like that

### Materials

❏ Pumpkin reproducible (page 26)

❏ "Pumpkin, Pumpkin" poem (page 30)

❏ brown construction paper

❏ scissors

❏ orange and yellow scrap paper

❏ glue

## Halloween Math

Give each child a Halloween Math reproducible, five pumpkin-shaped candies, and five black jelly beans. Explain that the pumpkin candies represent "pumpkins" and the jelly beans represent "bats." Tell a math story problem, and have children use the manipulatives to show the solution. For example, say *3 happy pumpkins are sitting on a fence. 4 bats fly over them. How many Halloween creatures are there in all?* Encourage children to place three pumpkin candies on the fence of the reproducible and four jelly beans in the space above the fence. Have children count all the items to determine the answer. Repeat the activity with a new set of numbers. Then, invite children to create their own story problem, record it on their reproducible, and draw pumpkins and bats to illustrate it.

### Materials

❏ Halloween Math reproducible (page 27)

❏ pumpkin-shaped candy

❏ black jelly beans

❏ crayons or markers

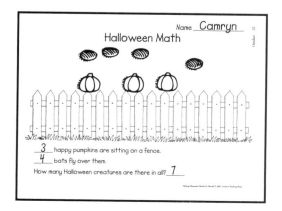

## Fall Leaves

### Materials

❏ Fall Leaves pattern (page 28)

❏ "Leaves" poem (page 30)

❏ card stock

❏ scissors

❏ food coloring (red, orange, yellow, and brown)

❏ small bowls of water

❏ coffee filters

❏ paper towels

Make several card stock copies of the Fall Leaves pattern, and copy a class set of the poem "Leaves." Cut out the leaf patterns. Place a few drops of each color of food coloring in separate bowls of water. Give each child a coffee filter. Invite children to dip the edges of their coffee filter in the colored water. The filter will absorb the colored water, creating a colorful pattern. Press their filters between paper towels. Once the filters have dried, have children trace a leaf pattern on their filter and cut it out. Hang the leaves in a window, or use them to enhance a fall bulletin board display. Then, place the leaves and the poem in children's memory books.

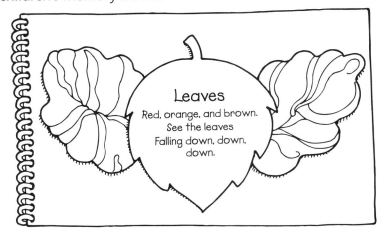

## The Spider in the Web

### Materials

❏ "The Spider in the Web" song (page 30)

❏ drawing paper

❏ black crayons or markers

❏ black ink pad

❏ glue

Lead a class discussion on spiders. Talk about the parts of a spider (e.g., eight legs, two body parts). Invite each child to draw a spiderweb on a piece of drawing paper. Then, have children stamp two fingerprints on their web to make a spider's body. Encourage them to draw legs and eyes to complete the spider. Have each child glue a copy of the poem "The Spider in the Web" on his or her paper.

# Pumpkin

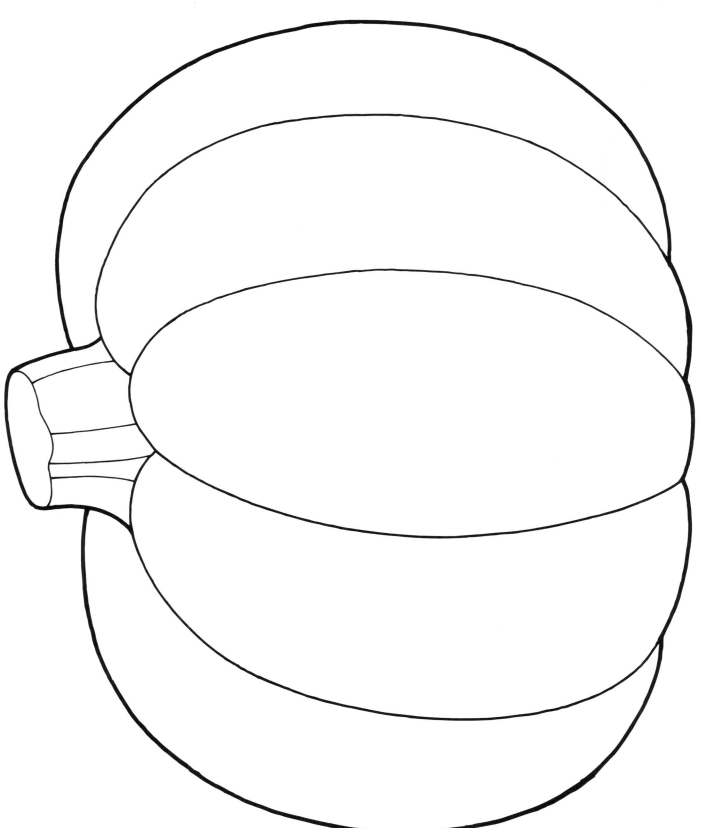

Name _____

_____ happy pumpkins are sitting on a fence.

_____ bats fly over them.

How many Halloween creatures are there in all? _____

# Fall Leaves

# October

(to the tune of "Are You Sleeping?")

It's October.
It's October.
Trick or treat.
Trick or treat.
Jack-o'-lanterns glowing.
Jack-o'-lanterns glowing.
Halloween!
Halloween!
Boo!

## Ghost

Paint the inside of each child's hand (palm and fingers) with white paint. Have children make an upside-down handprint on a piece of black paper. Invite them to dip one finger in black paint to make eyes and a mouth for their ghost.

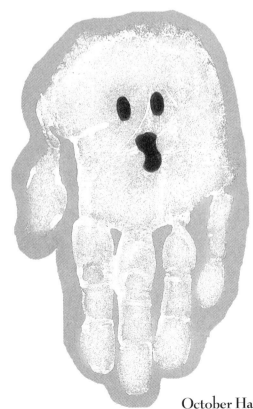

## Leaves

Red, orange, and brown.
See the leaves
Falling down, down,
down.

## Pumpkin, Pumpkin

Pumpkin, pumpkin
Round and fat,
Turn into a jack-o'-lantern
Just like that.

## The Spider in the Web
(to the tune of "The Farmer in the Dell")

The spider in the web,
The spider in the web,
Spin, spin, oh watch it spin,
The spider in the web.

This is how I look in October. I like when the leaves start to turn different colors and Halloween is here! I am going to be _____ for Halloween.

# NOVEMBER

There are so many wonderful teaching ideas and opportunities for children to express themselves in November, including the first Thanksgiving, Native Americans, and harvest time. You can teach children about corn and plan a classroom feast as a culminating activity.

## Literature Links

- *Arthur's Thanksgiving* by Marc Brown (Econo-Clad Books)

- *Corn* by Ann Burckhardt (Bridgestone Books)

- *Corn is Maize: The Gift of the Indians* by Aliki (Harper Trophy)

- *The First Thanksgiving* by Linda Hayward (Econo-Clad Books)

- *If You Sailed on the Mayflower in 1620* by Ann McGovern (Scholastic)

- *Thanksgiving Day* by Gail Gibbons (Holiday House)

## Thankful Turkeys

### Materials

- ❏ Turkey Feathers reproducible (page 37)
- ❏ construction paper (6 colors)
- ❏ scissors
- ❏ 4" x 5" (10 cm x 12.5 cm) brown paper rectangles
- ❏ 2½" x 11" (6.3 cm x 28 cm) red paper strips
- ❏ glue
- ❏ yellow scrap paper

Copy the Turkey Feathers reproducible on six colors of construction paper. (Each child will need one feather in each color.) Cut apart a set of feathers for each child. Invite children to brainstorm a list of things for which they are thankful. Write their responses on the chalkboard. Give each child a set of feathers, a brown paper rectangle, and a strip of red paper. Have children complete the sentence frame on each feather and then glue the feathers to the back of the brown rectangle. Show children how to roll their paper strip and glue it to the top of the brown rectangle to create the turkey's head. Invite children to use yellow scrap paper to make a beak, eyes, and feet and then glue them to the front of the turkey. Place the finished turkeys on a bulletin board titled *Give Thanks.*

## If I Sailed on the Mayflower

### Materials

- ❏ *If You Sailed on the Mayflower in 1620* by Ann McGovern
- ❏ Mayflower Suitcase reproducible (page 38)
- ❏ drawing paper
- ❏ crayons or markers

Read aloud *If You Sailed on the Mayflower in 1620.* Discuss the story with the class, and ask children what they would take with them if they sailed on the Mayflower. Have children write or dictate their sentence on the Mayflower Suitcase reproducible, and ask them to cut out their suitcase. Then, invite children to draw a large picture of themselves dressed as a pilgrim and cut it out. Display their drawings and suitcases on a bulletin board titled *If We Sailed on the Mayflower.*

## Mosaic Corncobs

### Materials

❏ Corn pattern
(page 39)

❏ card stock

❏ scissors

❏ yellow, brown,
and orange
construction
paper

❏ glue

❏ raffia

Make a card stock copy of the Corn pattern for each child, and have children cut out the corncob. Invite children to tear pieces of yellow, brown, and orange construction paper and glue them on their cob. Encourage children to overlap the paper and completely cover their cob. Tie raffia into bows, and glue a bow to the top of each cob. Display the corncobs on a fall bulletin board.

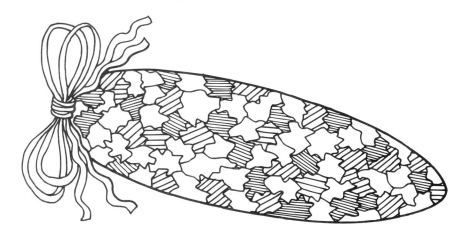

## Corn Counting

### Materials

❏ Corn pattern
(page 39)

❏ Corn Sentence
Strips reproducible
(page 40)

❏ card stock

❏ scissors

❏ yellow and green
construction paper

❏ glue

❏ corn kernels

Make several card stock copies of the Corn pattern, and make several copies of the Corn Sentence Strips reproducible. Cut out the corncob and leaf patterns, and cut apart the sentence strips. Have each child take turns tracing a corncob on yellow paper and two leaves on green paper and cut out the pieces. Tell children to glue a leaf on each side of their cob. Give each child a handful of corn kernels and a sentence strip. Name a number, and ask children to glue that many kernels on their cob. Have each child complete the sentence *I counted _____ kernels of corn*. Then, invite children to glue their sentence strip to one of their leaves.

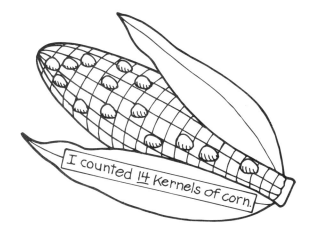

# Turkey Feathers

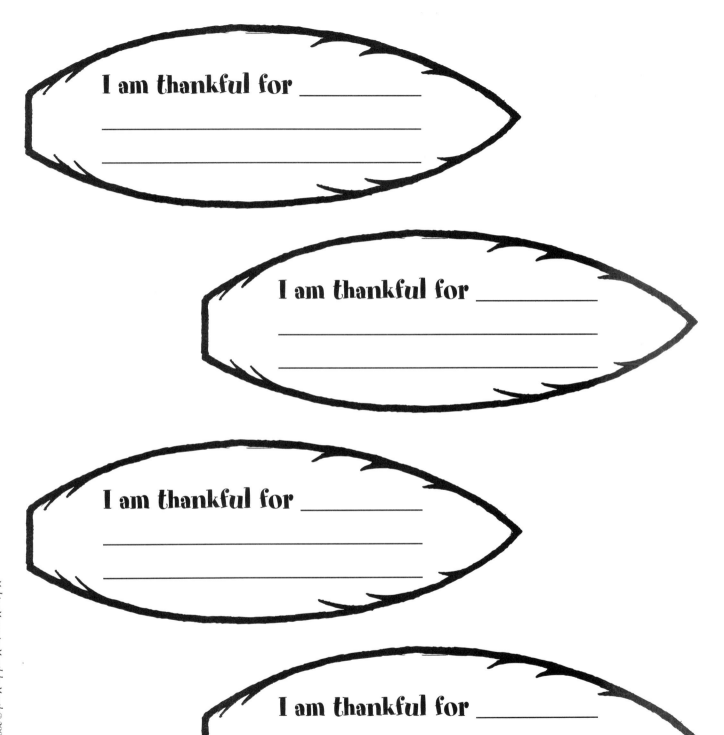

I am thankful for _____
_____
_____

I am thankful for _____
_____
_____

I am thankful for _____
_____
_____

I am thankful for _____
_____
_____

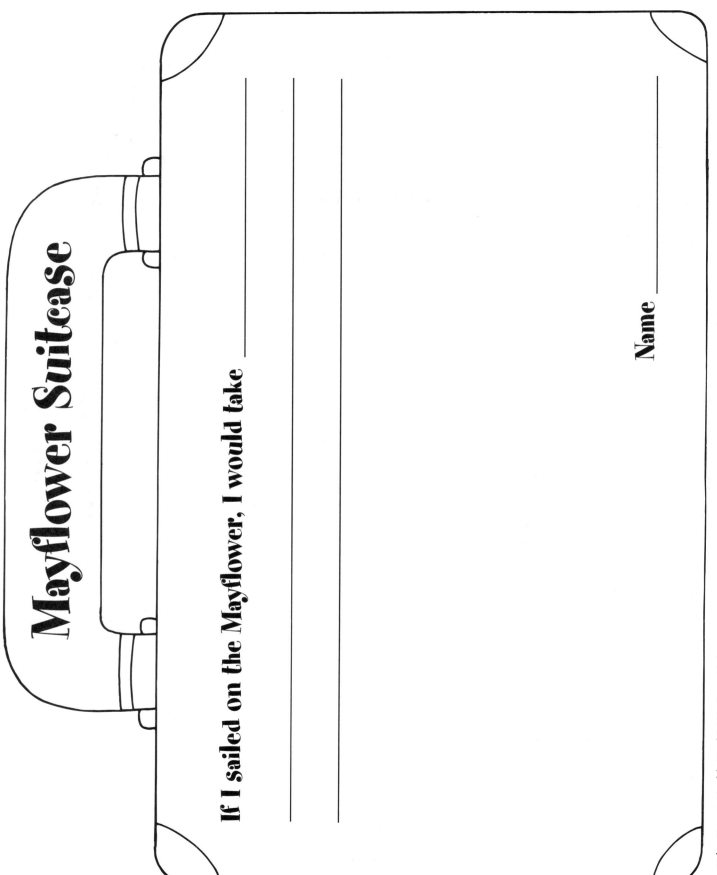

# Mayflower Suitcase

## If I sailed on the Mayflower, I would take

Name

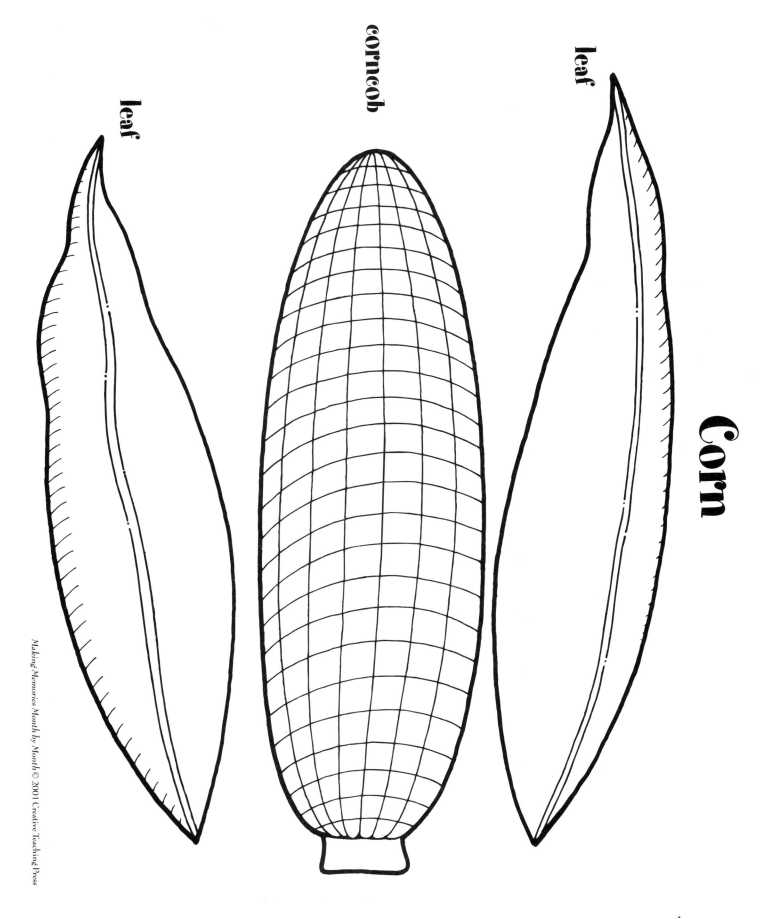

leaf

corncob

leaf

Corn

# Corn Sentence Strips

I counted _____ kernels of corn.

I counted _____ kernels of corn.

I counted _____ kernels of corn.

I counted _____ kernels of corn.

I counted _____ kernels of corn.

I counted _____ kernels of corn.

I counted _____ kernels of corn.

I counted _____ kernels of corn.

I counted _____ kernels of corn.

I counted _____ kernels of corn.

Making Memories Month by Month © 2001 Creative Teaching Press

# November

(to the tune of "Are You Sleeping?")

It's November.
It's November.
Let's give thanks.
Let's give thanks.
Pilgrims set the table.
Pilgrims set the table.
Indians brought the food.
Indians brought the food.

## Turkey

Paint the palm and thumb of each child's hand with brown paint. Paint the remaining fingers with green, red, orange, and yellow paint. Ask children to press their hand on a piece of white paper. Have them use red paint to make a wattle for their turkey and black paint to make an eye.

# Here Is a Turkey

Here is a turkey
With his tail spread wide.
He sees the farmer coming,
So he's trying to hide.
He runs across the barnyard,
Wobble, wobble, wobble.
Talking turkey talk,
Gobble, gobble, gobble.

# I Am Thankful

I am thankful for all I see
And everything that belongs to me.
I am thankful for my mom and dad
Who have given me all that I've had.
I am thankful for the food I eat
And the shoes that are on my feet.
I am thankful for so many things,
Especially the love my family brings.

*Making Memories Month by Month* © 2001 Creative Teaching Press

This is how I look in November. I am thankful

for _____

_____

# DECEMBER ......................

December is full of fun and excitement. There are many holidays in December, and people celebrate in many different ways. It is important to expose children to the different holidays and cultures. Introduce children to the various winter holidays (e.g., Hanukkah, Christmas, Las Posadas). Include a piece of holiday artwork and a brief description of the holiday (see page 52) on a December page in the memory book.

## Literature Links ................................

☆ *Christmas Around the World* by Mary K. Lankford (Mulberry Books)

☆ *Felix's Christmas Around the World* by Annette Langen (Abbeville Press)

☆ *The Legend of the Poinsettia* by Tomie dePaola (Putnam Publishing Group)

☆ *The Night of Las Posadas* by Tomie dePaola (Putnam Publishing Group)

☆ *Olive, the Other Reindeer* by J. Otto Seibold and Vivian Walsh (Chronicle Books)

☆ *Our Eight Nights of Hanukkah* by Michael J. Rosen (Holiday House)

## Christmas Tree Math

**Materials**

❑ Tree Math reproducible (page 49)

❑ small red and blue manipulatives (e.g., buttons, beads)

❑ crayons or markers

Give each child a Tree Math reproducible to use as a story mat and some red and blue manipulatives. Tell a math story problem, and have children use the manipulatives to show the solution. For example, say *There are two red ornaments and three blue ornaments on the tree. How many ornaments are there altogether?* Encourage children to place two red manipulatives and three blue manipulatives on their tree to find the answer. Repeat the activity with a new story problem. Then, have children create their own story problem, record it on their reproducible, and color their tree to illustrate it.

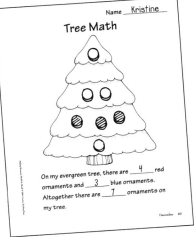

## Christmas—Reindeer

**Materials**

❑ brown and black construction paper

❑ scissors

❑ glue

For each child, trace one foot and both hands on brown construction paper. Ask children to cut out their tracings. Have them glue their hand cutouts to their foot cutout to create the antlers of a reindeer. Invite children to cut black construction paper to make a nose and eyes and then glue them to their reindeer.

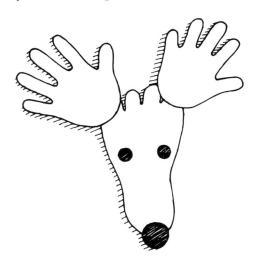

December 47

## Materials

❏ *The Legend of the Poinsettia* by Tomie dePaola

❏ Poinsettia pattern (page 50)

❏ scissors

❏ red and green tissue paper

❏ hole punch

❏ yellow and white construction paper

❏ paintbrushes

❏ small bowls of starch

# Las Posadas—Poinsettias

Copy and cut out the Poinsettia patterns. Use the patterns to trace for each child four to five red leaves on red tissue paper and two green leaves on green tissue paper. Cut out the tracings. Hole-punch enough yellow paper to make four to five cutouts for each child. Read aloud *The Legend of the Poinsettia*. Discuss the importance of poinsettias. Give each child a piece of white paper, a set of red and green leaves, and several yellow cutouts. Invite children to arrange their leaves on their paper to create a poinsettia. Have them use a paintbrush to cover their pieces with starch. (The starch will make the pieces stick to the paper.) Ask children to place their yellow cutouts in the center of their flower.

## Materials

❏ *Our Eight Nights of Hanukkah* by Michael J. Rosen

❏ Menorah reproducible (page 51)

❏ straws

❏ crayons or markers

❏ scissors

❏ glue

❏ orange yarn

# Hanukkah—Menorah

Read aloud *Our Eight Nights of Hanukkah*. Discuss the story with the class. Give each child a Menorah reproducible and three straws. Invite children to color their menorah. Have them cut their straws to make nine 2–3" (5–7.5 cm) pieces and then glue them to their menorah to create the candles. Have children glue bits of orange yarn to the top of each candle to create the flame. Have children number their candles from 1 to 9.

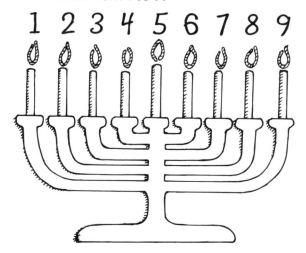

Name _____

# Tree Math

On my evergreen tree, there are _____ red ornaments and _____ blue ornaments. Altogether there are _____ ornaments on my tree.

# Poinsettia

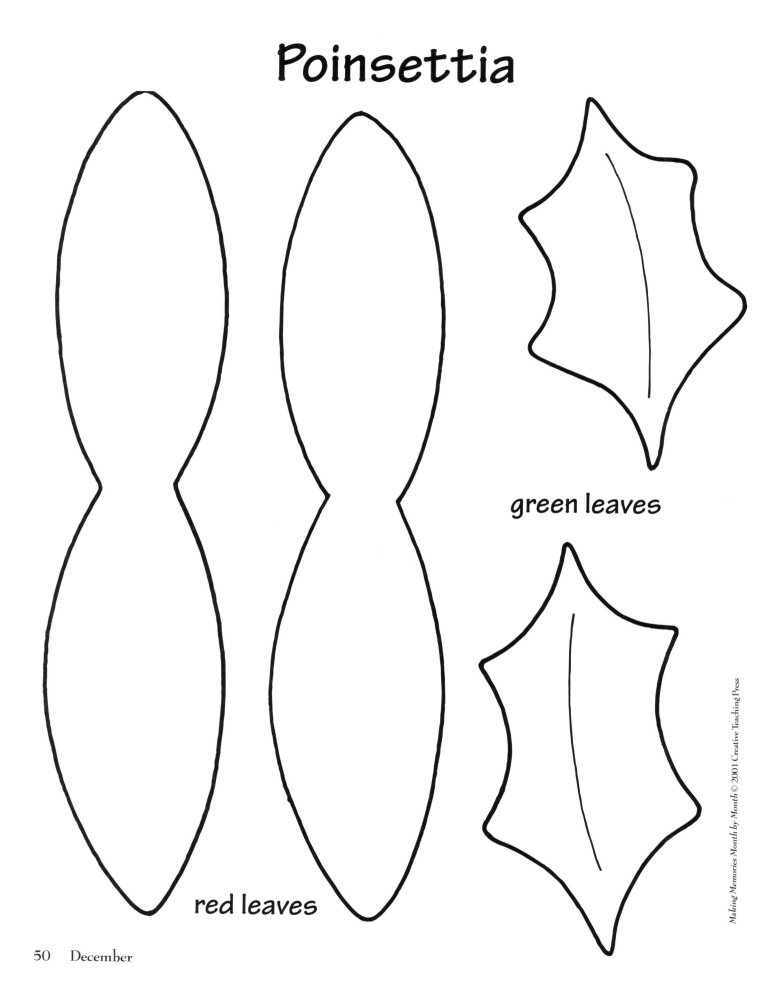

green leaves

red leaves

*Making Memories Month by Month* © 2001 Creative Teaching Press

**Menorah**

# Holidays around the World

## Mexico

The poinsettia came to the United States from Mexico. The people of Mexico call the plant Flor De La Noche Buena, which means Flower of the Holy Night. The poinsettia is a wild plant with tiny yellow flowers surrounded by beautiful red leaves (which look like petals).

## Israel

Jewish families celebrate Hanukkah, the Festival of Lights. They light candles on a menorah. There are nine candles on a menorah—one shamash (used to light the other candles) and one candle for each of the eight days of Hanukkah. Jewish families celebrate this holiday by singing, giving gifts, and eating special foods. Children play the dreidel game with their special tops.

## United States

Many families in the United States share holiday traditions that include Santa Claus. Families decorate a tree, hang stockings from their fireplaces, and anxiously await the arrival of Santa Claus on Christmas Eve.

*Making Memories Month by Month* © 2001 Creative Teaching Press

# December
### (to the tune of "Are You Sleeping?")

It's December.
It's December.
Decorate the tree.
Decorate the tree.
Mistletoe and holly.
Santa Claus is jolly.
Hear the bells.
Holiday bells.

## Santa

Paint the middle section of each child's palm with tan paint. Use red paint for the bottom section of the palm and the thumb. Paint the four fingers white. Have children make an upside-down handprint on a piece of colored paper. Invite them to use black paint to make the eyes and a nose.

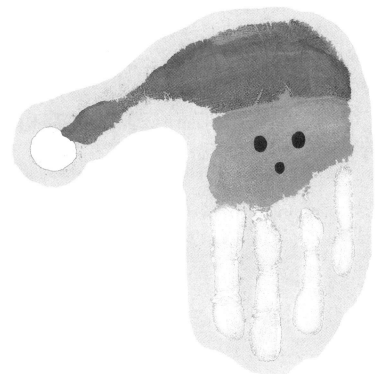

# Hanukkah

(to the tune of "Three Blind Mice")

Hanukkah, Hanukkah,
Eight special nights, nine special lights.
We light one candle for every night
To remember the miracle that was a great sight
When the oil lasted eight days and nights.
Oh, Hanukkah.

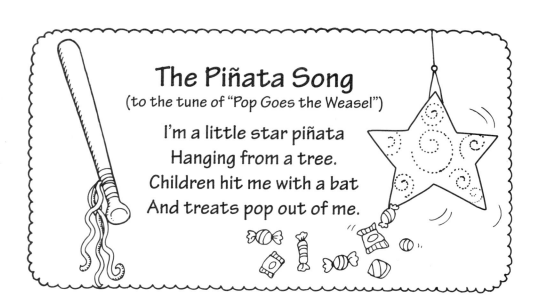

## The Piñata Song
(to the tune of "Pop Goes the Weasel")

I'm a little star piñata
Hanging from a tree.
Children hit me with a bat
And treats pop out of me.

*Making Memories Month by Month* © 2001 Creative Teaching Press

This is how I look in December. I love to

_____

_____

with my family during the holidays.

56    December Writing Paper

Making Memories Month by Month © 2001 Creative Teaching Press

# JANUARY

January is a great month for having winter fun that involves snow-men, mittens, New Year's Day, igloos, Eskimos, winter animal reports, and Martin Luther King, Jr. Day. It would be easy to dedicate the entire month to just a snow theme. For those who do not live where it snows, use your imagination to create some winter fun.

## Literature Links

☆ *The Biggest, Best Snowman* by Margery Cuyler (Scholastic)

☆ *The Jacket I Wear in the Snow* by Shirley Neitzel (Greenwillow Books)

☆ *The Mitten* by Jan Brett (Putnam Publishing Group)

☆ *A Picture Book of Martin Luther King, Jr.* by David Adler (Holiday House)

☆ *Snowballs* by Lois Ehlert (Harcourt)

☆ *The Snowman* by Raymond Briggs (Random House)

## Snowman Math

### Materials

- ❏ Snowmen reproducible (page 61)
- ❏ yarn
- ❏ crayons or markers
- ❏ glue
- ❏ small beans

Give each child a Snowmen reproducible and a piece of yarn. Invite children to color the face, draw a hat, and glue a yarn scarf on each snowman. Give each child a handful of small beans. Tell children to place three beans on one snowman and four beans on the other snowman. Ask them how many beans there are altogether. Encourage children to practice making different equations. Then, have children choose one equation, record it beneath their snowmen, and glue the beans on their snowmen to illustrate it.

## Snowman Glyphs

### Materials

- ❏ Snowman Sentence Frame reproducible (page 62)
- ❏ scissors
- ❏ sponges
- ❏ white, red, and green paint/ paintbrushes
- ❏ blue construction paper

Make several copies of the Snowman Sentence Frame reproducible, and cut apart the strips. Have each child use a sponge and white paint to sponge-paint a snowman on a piece of blue paper. Ask girls to paint a red scarf and boys to paint a green scarf on their snowman. Invite children to paint a button for each member of their family. Give each child a strip. Have children complete the sentence frames based on their snowman glyph. Use the information from the snowman glyphs to make a picture graph of how many boys and girls there are in the class. Display the graph and glyphs on a bulletin board.

## The Mitten

Copy a class set of the Mittens reproducible on white construction paper and a class set of the Left and Right reproducible. Read aloud *The Mitten*. Have children retell the story and act it out. Give each child a Mittens reproducible. Have children use crayons to decorate both mittens with the same design and then cut them out. Show children how to paint over their paper with watercolor paint. Give each child a Left and Right reproducible. Read the poem, and invite children to recite it. Have children trace their hands on the reproducible. Encourage them to number the fingers from 1 to 10. Ask children to label their hands *left* and *right*. Have them place their mittens on top of their traced hands. Use a brass fastener to attach each mitten to the reproducible.

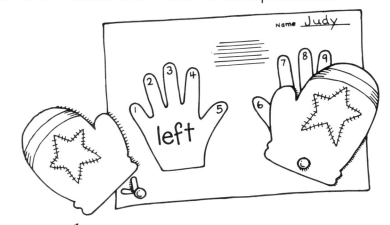

## Martin Luther King, Jr.

For each child, cut out a cloud shape from white construction paper. Read aloud *A Picture Book of Martin Luther King, Jr.* Discuss the life of Martin Luther King, Jr. and the important things that he did. Give each child a cloud cutout, and encourage children to write or dictate what their "dream" is for making the world a better place. Have them draw a picture to go with their sentence.

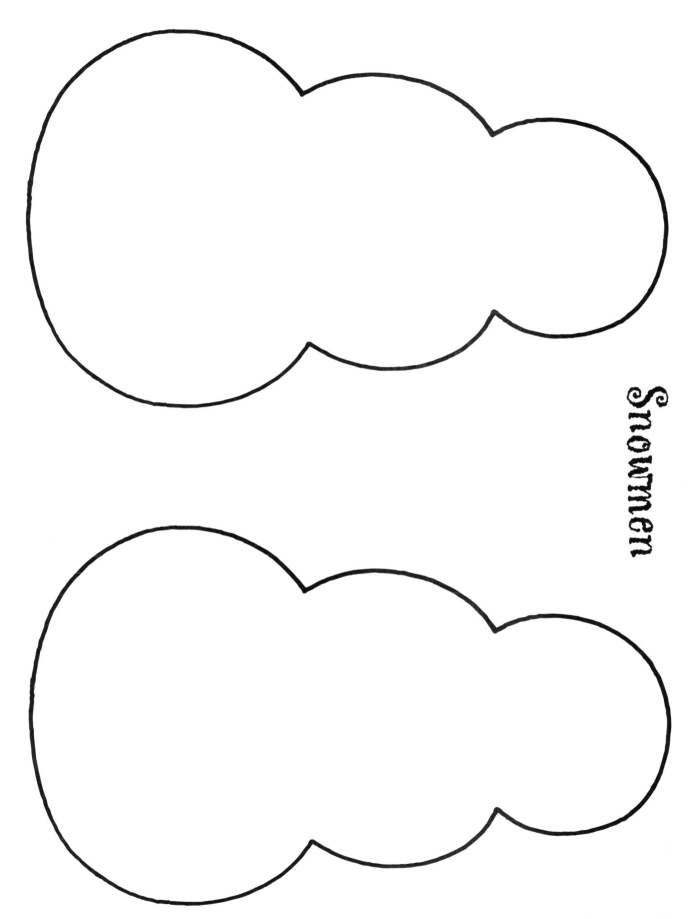

Snowmen

Making Memories Month by Month © 2001 Creative Teaching Press

# Snowman Sentence Frame

- - - - - - - - - - - - - - - - - - - - - - - - - - - - - - - - - - - - - - - - -

My snowman's scarf is _____.

I am a _____,

and I have _____people in my family.

- - - - - - - - - - - - - - - - - - - - - - - - - - - - - - - - - - - - - - - - -

My snowman's scarf is _____.

I am a _____,

and I have _____people in my family.

- - - - - - - - - - - - - - - - - - - - - - - - - - - - - - - - - - - - - - - - -

My snowman's scarf is _____.

I am a _____,

and I have _____people in my family.

- - - - - - - - - - - - - - - - - - - - - - - - - - - - - - - - - - - - - - - - -

My snowman's scarf is _____.

I am a _____,

and I have _____people in my family.

*Making Memories Month by Month* © 2001 Creative Teaching Press

**Mittens**

# Left and Right

Left and right.
Left and right.
They go together like day and night.
When it's cold and when it's snowy,
My mittens keep my hands warm and cozy!

*Making Memories Month by Month* © 2001 Creative Teaching Press

# January
(to the tune of "Are You Sleeping?")

January.
January.
Happy New Year!
Happy New Year!
Icicles and snowflakes.
Hot cocoa and snowmen.
Winter's here.
Winter's here.

## Winter Tree

Paint each child's palm, fingers, and wrist with brown paint. Have children press their hand and wrist on a piece of light blue paper. Then, invite them to dip their fingers in white paint and dab snow on their tree.

January Handprint Idea   65

# I'm a Little Snowman

I'm a little snowman,
Short and fat.
Here are my mittens.
Here is my hat.
When the sun comes out
I melt away.
See you next year
On a snowy day!

# My Snowman

I made a little snowman
On a cold and wintry day.
I made a little snowman
In hopes that he could play.
I gave him two eyes and a long carrot nose
And a nice little mouth for talking—I suppose.
I waited, and I waited just to hear him say,
"What would you like to play today?"

Making Memories Month by Month © 2001 Creative Teaching Press

This is how I look in January. This New Year I want to learn how to _____

_____

_____

_____

*Making Memories Month by Month* © 2001 Creative Teaching Press

# FEBRUARY ......................................

February is an exciting and fun time for children to send and receive valentines, guess if the groundhog will see its shadow, and learn about Abraham Lincoln and George Washington. It is also a good month to study animals and their wintertime behaviors. Even very young children can learn and write about what different animals do in winter.

## Literature Links ....................................

☆ *Abe Lincoln's Hat* by Martha Brenner (Random House)

☆ *Celebrating Valentine's Day* by Kimberly Roark (Creative Teaching Press)

☆ *I Love You, A Rebus Poem* by Jean Marzollo (Cartwheel Books®)

☆ *It's Valentine's Day* by Jack Prelutsky (Econo-Clad Books)

☆ *Roses Are Pink, Your Feet Really Stink* by Diane deGroat (Mulberry Books)

☆ *Tacky the Penguin* by Helen Lester (Houghton Mifflin)

## If I Were President ...

### Materials

- ❏ tape
- ❏ black construction paper
- ❏ overhead projector
- ❏ scissors
- ❏ lined paper
- ❏ glue

Have a child sit in a chair near a wall. Tape a piece of black construction paper behind the child's head. Make a silhouette of the child by using an overhead projector to cast light on his or her face and tracing the shadow on the black paper. Repeat the procedure for each child in the class. Invite children to cut out their silhouette. Ask children what they would do if they were the president of the United States. Have each child write or dictate his or her response, and glue it to the back of his or her silhouette.

### Materials

- ❏ *Abe Lincoln's Hat* by Martha Brenner
- ❏ Abe Lincoln's Hat reproducible (page 73)
- ❏ scissors
- ❏ top hat (optional)
- ❏ camera/film (optional)

## Abe Lincoln's Hat

Read aloud *Abe Lincoln's Hat*. Discuss with children the things Abe Lincoln carried in his hat. Give each child an Abe Lincoln's Hat reproducible, and have children complete the sentence frame with what they would carry in their hat. Ask them to cut out their hat. If you have access to a top hat, take a picture of each child wearing the hat. Display the completed reproducibles and photos on a bulletin board.

## Valentine Penguin

Make several card stock copies of the Penguin patterns, and copy a class set of the poem "Valentine." Cut out the patterns. Have children take turns tracing a penguin outline pattern on black construction paper, the body pattern on white paper, and two feet patterns on orange construction paper. Invite children to cut out their tracings and then glue the body and feet on the black outline to make a penguin. Have them fold their penguin in half lengthwise and cut a small diagonal slit above the oval to make a nose. Ask children to place two white paper reinforcements on the penguin to make eyes. Have children glue the poem to the front of their penguin. Have the class recite the poem together.

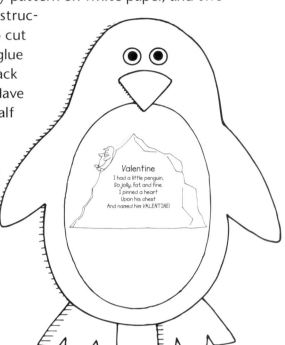

Valentine
I had a little penguin,
So jolly, fat and fine.
I pinned a heart
Upon his chest
And named him VALENTINE!

### Materials

❏ Penguin patterns (pages 74–75)

❏ "Valentine" poem (page 78)

❏ card stock

❏ scissors

❏ black, white, and orange construction paper

❏ glue

❏ white paper reinforcements

## I Love

Make copies of the I Love . . . reproducible, and cut apart the boxes. Have each child cut out a large heart from construction paper. (The heart needs to be big enough to place a reproducible box on.) Ask children to cover their heart with pieces of pink and red paper. Give each child a box, and invite children to write people's names or items on the blank lines to complete the frames. For example, a child could write I love _my mom_. I love _my dad_. I love _pizza_. But I love _my family_ most of all. Have children glue their box on top of their paper heart.

I love __my mom__
I love __my dog__
I love __pizza__
But I love __my family__ most of all.

### Materials

❏ I Love . . . reproducible (page 76)

❏ scissors

❏ construction paper

❏ pink and red construction (or tissue) paper scraps

❏ glue

# Abe Lincoln's Hat

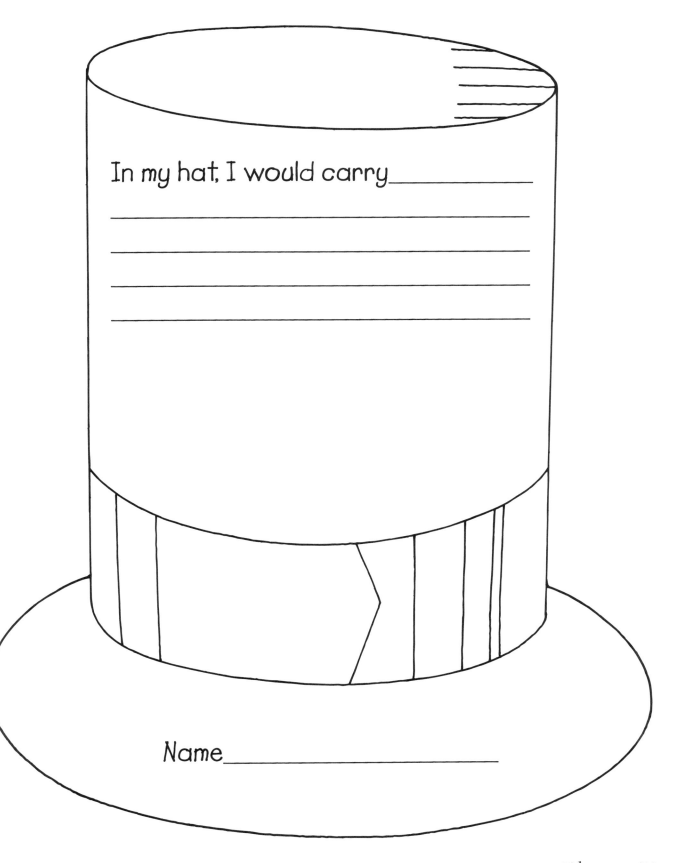

In my hat, I would carry_____

_____

_____

_____

_____

Name_____

# Penguin

# Penguin

body

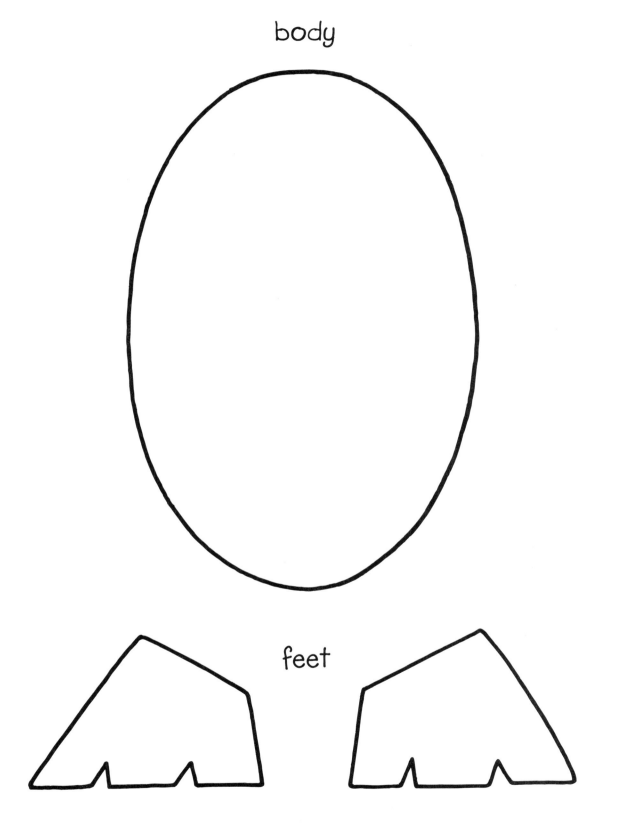

feet

# I Love . . .

I love _____.

I love _____.

I love _____.

But I love _____ most of all.

I love _____.

I love _____.

I love _____.

But I love _____ most of all.

# February

(to the tune of "Are You Sleeping?")

February.
February.
Groundhog's Day.
Groundhog's Day.
Washington and Lincoln.
Valentines and sweethearts.
I love you! I love you!

## Heart

Paint children's hands with red paint. Ask them to tightly hold together their fingers and thumb. Have children make two upside-down handprints to form a heart on a piece of white paper. Invite them to dip their fingers in pink paint and add a dotted border around their heart.

Making Memories Month by Month © 2001 Creative Teaching Press

# Valentine

I had a little penguin,
So jolly, fat, and fine.
I pinned a heart
Upon his chest
And named him VALENTINE!

# Abraham Lincoln

(to the tune of "Three Blind Mice")

Abraham Lincoln.
Abraham Lincoln.
Our 16th president.
Our 16th president.
He helped make the U.S. a great country.
He saved the union and made slaves free.
He was as honest and brave as he could be.
That's Abraham Lincoln!

*Making Memories Month by Month* © 2001 Creative Teaching Press

This is how I look in February. My family is special. I love them because _____

_____

_____

_____

Making Memories Month by Month © 2001 Creative Teaching Press

# MARCH

There is so much to do in March. It's the perfect month to learn about spring, weather, baby animals, and rainbows. It's a wonderful time for science activities and opportunities for children to write across the curriculum. At this time, younger children are gaining confidence with independent writing. Be sure to include a writing sample on this month's pages.

## Literature Links

☆ *First Day of Spring* by Sharon Gordon (Troll Communications)

☆ *Hopper Hunts for Spring* by Marcus Pfister (North-South Books)

☆ *How Do You Know It's Spring?* by Allan Fowler (Children's Press)

☆ *Jamie O'Rourke and the Big Potato* by Tomie dePaola (Putnam Publishing Group)

☆ *The Rainbow Fish* by Marcus Pfister (North-South Books)

☆ *St. Patrick's Day* by Gail Gibbons (Holiday House)

## Rainbow Fish

**Materials**

❏ *The Rainbow Fish* by Marcus Pfister

❏ Fish Sentence Frame reproducible (page 85)

❏ blue paper

❏ scissors

❏ paper plates

❏ stapler

❏ paint/paintbrushes

❏ glue

❏ shiny paper

Make copies of the Fish Sentence Frame reproducible on blue paper, and cut the copies in half. Read aloud *The Rainbow Fish*. Invite children to make their own rainbow fish. Have children cut a triangular wedge from a paper plate to create a mouth and then staple the wedge to the opposite end of the plate to serve as a tail. Invite children to paint their fish and then glue on a piece of shiny paper to be the special gill. Give each child a sentence frame to complete. Display the fish and the completed sentence frames on a bulletin board titled *A Rainbow of Friends*.

## Pot of Gold

**Materials**

❏ Pot of Gold reproducible (page 86)

❏ scissors

❏ glue

❏ crayons or markers

Give each child a Pot of Gold reproducible. Read the poem with the class. Ask children how old they are and how old they will be on their next birthday. Have them cut apart the strip of coins and glue in the pot the number of coins that matches the age they will be on their next birthday. For example, a five-year-old would glue six coins in the pot. Ask children to color the rainbow.

## I'm a Little Leprechaun

### Materials

❑ Leprechaun pattern (page 87)

❑ "I'm a Little Leprechaun" song (page 89)

❑ card stock

❑ scissors

❑ dark green, orange, and light green construction paper

❑ glue

❑ sentence strips

❑ stapler

❑ camera/film

Make several card stock copies of the Leprechaun patterns, and cut them out. Make a class set of the song "I'm a Little Leprechaun." Have each child trace a hat on a folded piece of dark green paper, a beard on a folded piece of orange paper, and a shamrock on light green paper and then cut out the pieces. Ask children to glue the hat and beard to a sentence strip so that the hat extends above the strip and the beard extends below it. Invite children to glue the shamrock to their hat. Staple each child's sentence strip together to fit his or her head. Invite children to chant the song and wear their hat. Take a photo of each child as a leprechaun. Include the photo and a copy of the song in each child's scrapbook.

## Fly, Robin, Fly

### Materials

❑ scissors

❑ light blue construction paper

❑ drawing paper

❑ crayons or pastels

❑ glue

❑ brown tissue paper

❑ yellow construction paper

Cut out ovals (robin's eggs) from light blue construction paper. Write a letter on each egg. (Be sure that the first letter of each child's first name appears on an egg.) Have each child draw a circle on drawing paper and color the top half dark brown and the bottom half reddish brown. Ask children to cut out their circle, and invite them to glue small brown tissue paper strips to the top half to add texture. Have them cut out a yellow diamond-shaped beak, fold it in half, and glue it on the circle. Invite children to cut out yellow construction paper legs and eyes and glue them on their "robin." Scatter the eggs on the floor, and have children "fly" their robin to the egg with the first letter of their first name. After the activity, hang the robins from the ceiling to welcome spring.

# Fish Sentence Frame

**Rainbow fish was a good friend. I'm a good friend because** _____

_____

**Rainbow fish was a good friend. I'm a good friend because** _____

_____

# Pot of Gold

Name _____

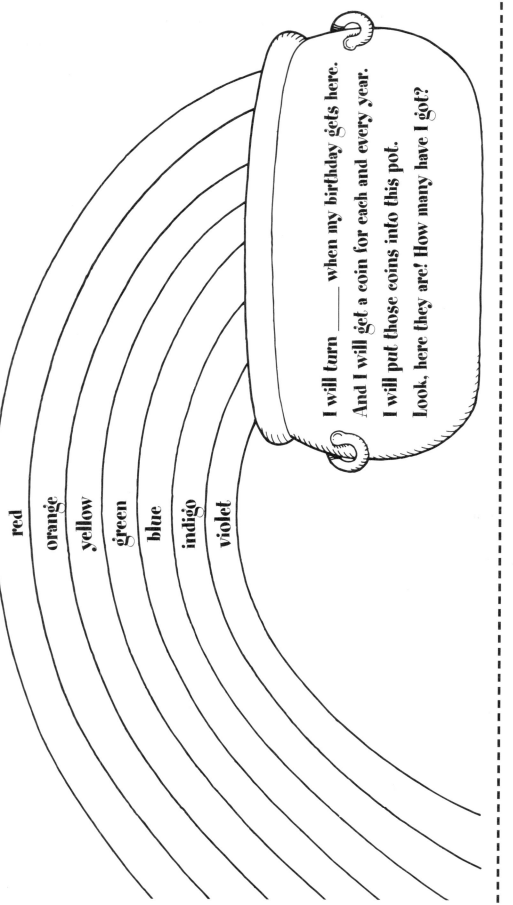

red
orange
yellow
green
blue
indigo
violet

I will turn _____ when my birthday gets here.
And I will get a coin for each and every year.
I will put those coins into this pot.
Look, here they are! How many have I got?

*Making Memories Month by Month* © 2001 Creative Teaching Press

# Leprechaun

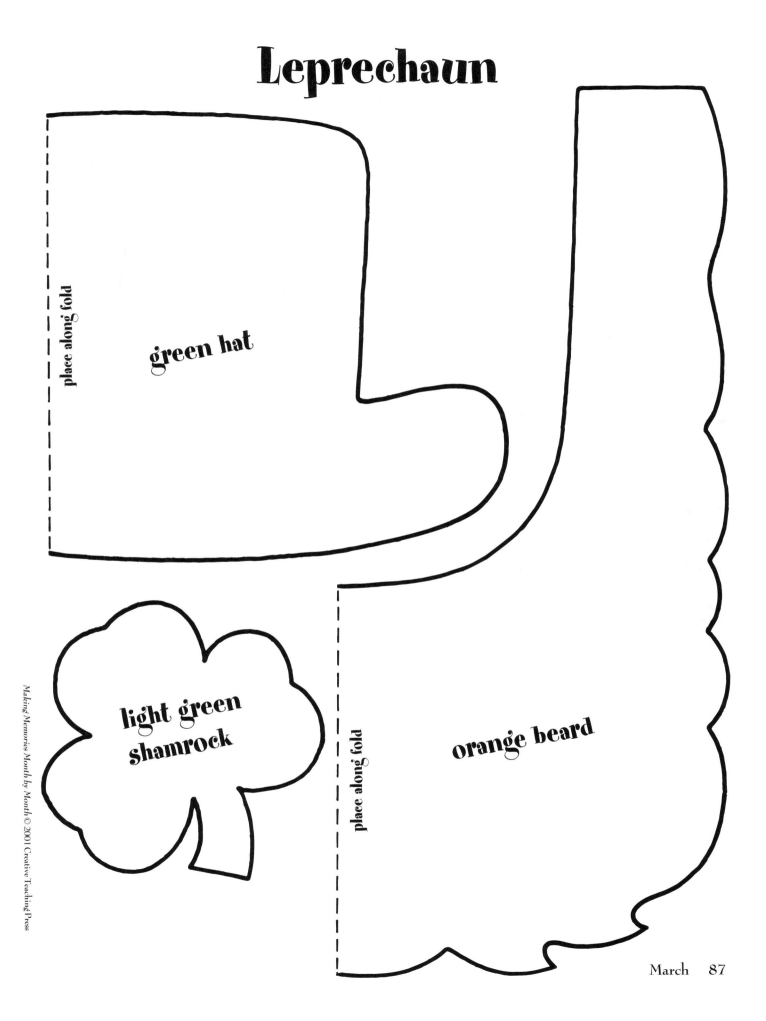

place along fold

green hat

light green shamrock

place along fold

orange beard

# March

(to the tune of "Are You Sleeping?")

It is March.
It is March.
Windy days, kite at play.
Leprechauns and shamrocks.
Leprechauns and shamrocks.
Spring is here.
Spring is here.

## Shamrock

Paint children's hands with green paint. Ask children to tightly hold together their fingers and thumb. Have them make three upside-down handprints to form a shamrock on a piece of white paper. (Note: Repaint one of their hands so they can make the third print.)

# The Rainbow

When I grow up, I will someday,
Paint a rainbow that will stay,
I'll climb upon a ladder high
And paint a rainbow in the sky.

# I'm a Little Leprechaun

(to the tune of "I'm a Little Teapot")

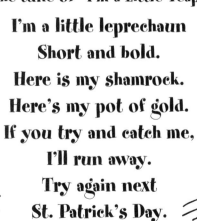

I'm a little leprechaun
Short and bold.
Here is my shamrock.
Here's my pot of gold.
If you try and catch me,
I'll run away.
Try again next
St. Patrick's Day.

This is how I look in March. If I were a
leprechaun, I would _____

_____

_____

_____

*Making Memories Month by Month* © 2001 Creative Teaching Press

*Making Memories Month by Month* © 2001 Creative Teaching Press

# APRIL

April is a great month to teach about the signs of spring. Baby animals, eggs, bunnies, and planting all lend themselves to projects for the memory books. Also teach children about farms this month.

## Literature Links

☆ *Barn Dance* by Bill Martin, Jr. and John Archambault (Henry Holt and Company)

☆ *The Earth and I* by Frank Asch (Harcourt)

☆ *Hopper* by Marcus Pfister (North-South Books)

☆ *The Runaway Bunny* by Margaret Wise Brown (HarperCollins)

☆ *Spot Goes to the Farm* by Eric Hill (Puffin)

☆ *The Wump World* by Bill Peet (Houghton Mifflin)

## You're a Good Egg

Write a letter asking parents to complete the reproducible by writing why their child is special. Make copies of the letter, and attach a letter to a Good Egg reproducible. Have each child take home the reproducible and letter. Encourage children to color the reproducible egg. Have children return the completed egg to school. Have children share with the class what parents wrote. Display the eggs on a bulletin board titled *You're a Good Egg*.

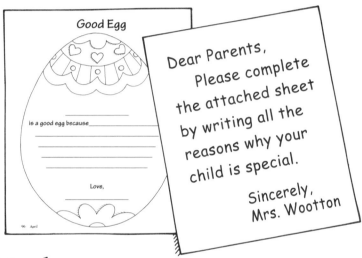

## Farm Mural

Read aloud *Spot Goes to the Farm*. Discuss with the class the baby animals in the book. Divide the class into small groups of four or five. Invite each group to paint a mural of a mother farm animal and its children (e.g., a pig and piglets, a horse and foals). Hang the murals on a wall. Take a few photos of each group standing in front of their mural. Place a photo in each child's scrapbook.

## Bunny Mask

Invite each child to make a bunny mask. Have children cut out rabbit ears, eyes, nose, mouth, and whiskers from construction paper and glue them onto a paper plate. Glue a copy of the poem on the back of each child's plate. Tape a tongue depressor or ruler to the back of each plate. Have children hold their mask in front of their face as they recite the poem.

### Materials

- ❏ "Bunnies" poem (page 99)
- ❏ scissors
- ❏ pink, white, and black construction paper
- ❏ glue
- ❏ paper plates
- ❏ tape
- ❏ tongue depressor or ruler

## Helping Our World—Earth Day

Read aloud *The Wump World*. Discuss the story, and then ask children what the Wumps could do after the Pollutions left their planet. Have children brainstorm ways that they could clean up and care for the environment. Give each child a Cleaning Up Our World reproducible. Invite children to color and cut out the reproducible. Have children glue their completed reproducible to a paper bag. Take the class on a walk around the school. Encourage children to pick up trash and place it in their bag. Take photos of the children during the walk. Then, have children dump the trash from their small bag into a large trash can. Have children write about the experience on an April frame, and place it and a photo in the scrapbooks.

### Materials

- ❏ *The Wump World* by Bill Peet
- ❏ Cleaning Up Our World reproducible (page 97)
- ❏ April frame (page 102)
- ❏ crayons or markers
- ❏ scissors
- ❏ glue
- ❏ small paper bag
- ❏ camera/film

# Good Egg

_____

is a good egg because_____

_____

_____

_____

_____

Love,

_____

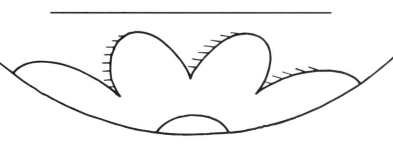

# Cleaning Up Our World

# April

(to the tune of "Are You Sleeping?")

It is April.
It is April.
Rainy days.
Rainy days.
Playing tricks so funny.
Eggs and Easter Bunny.
Easter time.
Easter time.

## Bunny

Paint children's palm and four fingers with white paint. Have children position their fingers so that their pinky and ring fingers are touching and their middle and index fingers are touching. Ask them to press their hand on a piece of colored paper. Invite children to use black paint to make eyes, a nose, a mouth, and whiskers for their bunny.

Making Memories Month by Month © 2001 Creative Teaching Press

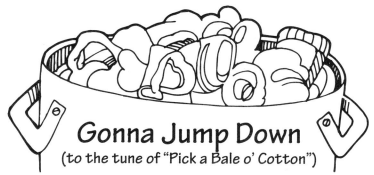

## Gonna Jump Down

*(to the tune of "Pick a Bale o' Cotton")*

Gonna jump down, turn around, pick a bit o' litter.
Gonna jump down, turn around, pick a bit a day.
Gonna jump down, turn around, pick a bit o' litter.
Gonna jump down, turn around, throw some trash away.

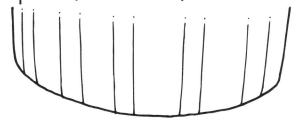

## Bunnies

Bunnies here,
Bunnies there,
Bunnies, bunnies,
Everywhere!

This is how I look in April. Spring break was

fun. My family and I _____

_____

_____

*Making Memories Month by Month* © 2001 Creative Teaching Press

# MAY

A lot is going on in May. Many schools have their Open House during this month. Teach children about flowers, insects, caterpillars, birds, and signs of spring. Invite them to study baby chicks and observe their birth and growth.

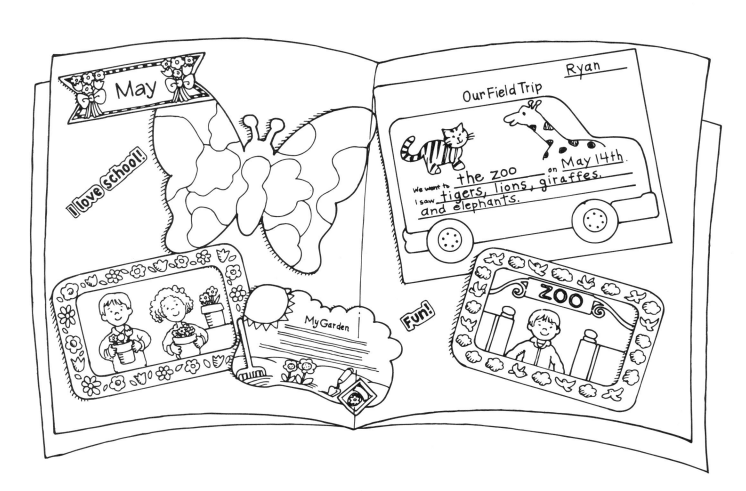

## Literature Links

☆ *Mama, Do You Love Me?* by Barbara Joose (Chronicle Books)

☆ *The Reason for a Flower* by Ruth Heller (Paper Star)

☆ *A Seed Is a Promise* by Claire Merrill (Scholastic)

☆ *The Tiny Seed* by Eric Carle (Simon & Schuster)

☆ *The Very Hungry Caterpillar* by Eric Carle (Philomel)

☆ *What Mommies Do Best* by Laura Numeroff (Simon & Schuster)

## Materials

- ❏ Butterfly reproducible (page 106)
- ❏ construction paper (assorted colors)
- ❏ scissors
- ❏ eyedroppers
- ❏ bottles of tempera paint
- ❏ lined writing paper

## Butterflies

Copy a class set of the Butterfly reproducible on colored construction paper. Discuss symmetry with the class. Give each child a reproducible, and have children cut out the butterfly. Have children take turns using the eyedroppers to place drops of paint on one side of the butterfly. Invite them to fold the butterfly in half and press down on the paper. Invite children to open their paper, and talk about how their butterfly is symmetrical. Have children write or dictate a story about their butterfly. Display the butterflies and stories on a bulletin board.

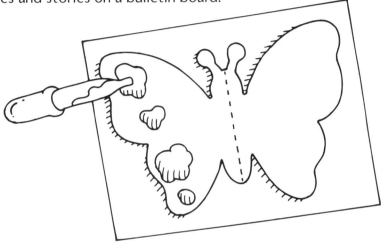

## Materials

- ❏ "Mother's Day" poem (page 109)
- ❏ chart paper
- ❏ scissors
- ❏ wallpaper or wrapping paper scraps
- ❏ glue
- ❏ drawing paper
- ❏ crayons or markers
- ❏ paint (assorted colors)

## Flowers for Mom

Write the poem "Mother's Day" on chart paper. Read the poem together as a class. Invite each child to cut a wallpaper or wrapping paper scrap into the shape of a vase. Have children glue their vase onto the bottom half of a piece of drawing paper. Ask children to draw lines to make the branches of the flowers. Then, have them dip their finger in different colors of paint to make the blooms on their paper. Have children glue a copy of the poem to their picture.

## Will You Love Me If?

### Materials

- ❏ *Mama, Do You Love Me?* by Barbara Joose
- ❏ Will You Love Me? reproducible (page 107)
- ❏ lined paper
- ❏ glue
- ❏ children's photos
- ❏ crayons or markers
- ❏ cotton

Read aloud *Mama, Do You Love Me?* Give each child a Will You Love Me? reproducible. Have children complete the sentence frame (e.g., *Will you love me if I accidently spill milk on the floor?*). Have children take home their completed reproducible and a piece of lined paper. Tell children to ask their father or mother to read the reproducible and then write his or her response on the lined paper. Have them bring both papers to school on the following day. Glue a photo of each child on the face area of his or her reproducible. Ask children to color their reproducible and then glue cotton (fur) to the coat. Invite them to share their completed reproducible and parent's response with the class.

## Painted Salt Flowers

### Materials

- ❏ 8¹⁄₂" x 11" (21.5 cm x 28 cm) sheets of black construction paper
- ❏ small paper plates
- ❏ tempera paint/ paintbrushes
- ❏ salt

Discuss with the class how mixing white paint with another color of paint will result in a lighter, softer color of paint. Give each child a sheet of black paper and a paper plate. Have children choose one color of paint and pour some on their plate. Invite them to mix in some white paint. For example, a child could mix green paint with white paint to make a mint green color. Invite children to use their paint to create a picture of a flower on the black paper. While the paint is wet, have children shake some salt over their painting. The salt will stick to the paint and make the flower "sparkle." When the paint is dry, have children hold up their painting. Chant the verse below, and have children stand up when their color is mentioned. Repeat the verse with new colors until all children have had a chance to stand up and share their picture.

(to the tune of "Goodnight Ladies")
*Stand up **yellow** flowers.*
*Stand up **yellow** flowers.*
*Stand up **yellow** flowers*
*So we can look at you.*

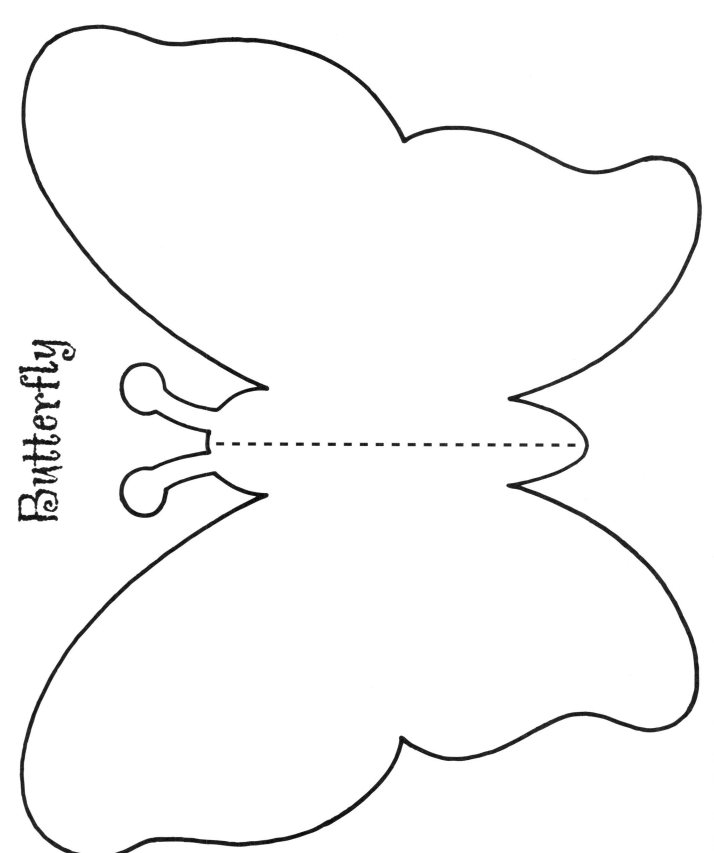

Butterfly

*Making Memories Month by Month* © 2001 Creative Teaching Press

# Will You Love Me?

Will you love me if _____

_____?

# May

(to the tune of "Are You Sleeping?")

It is May.
It is May.
Flowers grow.
Flowers grow.
Summer is near.
Summer is near.
I love you,
Mother dear.

## Swan

Paint children's entire hand with white paint. Have children make a sideways handprint on a piece of colored paper. (Have them extend their thumb so it is sticking straight up when they press down their hand.) Have children use orange paint to make a beak and black paint to make an eye on their swan.

## Mother's Day

I see flowers blooming bright in the sun.
How will I choose just the right one?
Mother's Day is coming, and it must be right
To say "I love you" with flowers so bright!

## My Garden

This is my garden. I'll rake it with care.
Here are the flower seeds I'll plant in there.
The sun will shine and the rain will fall.
And my garden will blossom and grow straight and tall.

# Open House

This is how I look in May. We have been getting ready for Open House. I can't wait to show my family _____

_____

_____

Making Memories Month by Month © 2001 Creative Teaching Press

# J JUNE ...............................................................

If your school follows a traditional school schedule, then June brings the school year to an end. Include summer plans, special letters to the children, autograph pages, pages for awards, and goals for the next year on the last pages of your memory books.

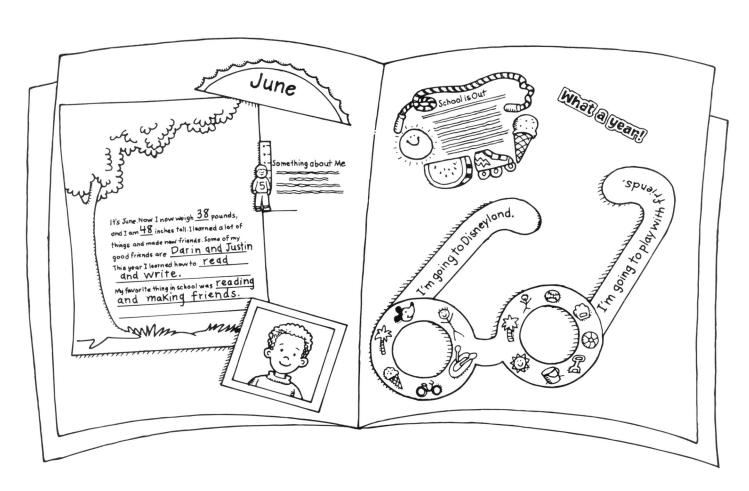

## Literature Links .........................................................

☆ *Arthur's Family Vacation* by Marc Brown (Econo-Clad Books)

☆ *Beach Play* by Marsha Hayles (Henry Holt and Company)

☆ *The Best Vacation Ever* by Stuart J. Murphy (HarperCollins)

☆ *Curious Kids Go on Vacation: Another Big Book of Words* by Heloise Antoine (Peachtree Publishers)

☆ *How I Spent My Summer Vacation* by Mark Teague (Econo-Clad Books)

☆ *A Perfect Father's Day* by Eve Bunting (Houghton Mifflin)

## Materials

❏ Watermelon Seeds reproducible (page 116)

❏ watermelon slices

❏ paper plates

❏ glue

## Watermelon Seeds

Give each child a slice of watermelon and a Watermelon Seeds reproducible. Ask children to guess how many seeds are in their slice and then write their estimate in the first sentence on their reproducible. Let children eat their watermelon and count the seeds. Invite them to glue their seeds on the reproducible and complete the second sentence frame. Discuss with children the concept of more or less by saying *If you have more (or less) than **6** seeds, **stand up**.* Change the number and action (e.g., *If you have less than 9 seeds, **jump up and down**),* and repeat the activity.

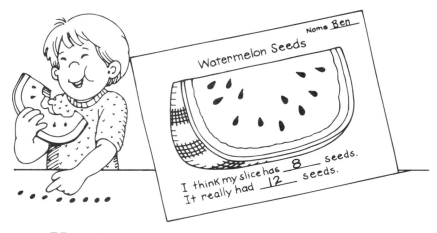

## Materials

❏ Glasses reproducible (page 117)

❏ crayons or markers

## Summer Vacation

Have children brainstorm things they would like to do over summer vacation. Record their responses on the chalkboard. Give each child a Glasses reproducible. Invite children to write or dictate on each arm of the glasses a sentence about something they would like to do over vacation. Encourage children to decorate the rims of the glasses.

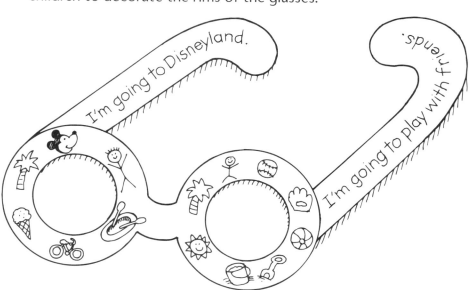

## Buckets of Shells

### Materials

- ❏ Beach Bucket reproducible (page 118)
- ❏ resealable plastic bags
- ❏ uncooked pasta shells
- ❏ rubbing alcohol
- ❏ food coloring (2 colors)
- ❏ newspaper
- ❏ crayons or markers
- ❏ scissors
- ❏ glue

Fill two resealable plastic bags about three-quarters full with uncooked pasta shells. Pour into each bag one capful of rubbing alcohol and a few drops of one color of food coloring. Securely seal and shake each bag until all the pasta shells are colored. The alcohol will help the color "set" on the shells. Spread the pasta shells out on several layers of newspaper to dry. Once the pasta is dry, give each child ten shells, five of each color, and a Beach Bucket reproducible to color and cut out. Have children sort the shells and use them to create math addition problems. Invite children to glue shells on the top of the beach bucket to create a math equation and then write it on the side of the bucket.

## My Dad

### Materials

- ❏ My Dad reproducible (page 119)
- ❏ scissors
- ❏ tan or white construction paper
- ❏ colored pencils
- ❏ glue
- ❏ yarn

Cut out circles (approximately 6" [15 cm] diameter) from tan or white construction paper. Give each child a My Dad reproducible and a circle. Have children complete the sentence frames. Allow children to write or dictate their own responses (e.g., *My dad is 2 feet tall*). Invite them to use colored pencils to lightly color and decorate the tie. Have children cut out the tie and glue it to their circle. Ask them to make a face on their circle and glue on yarn for hair.

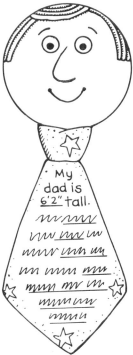

# Watermelon Seeds

I think my slice has _____ seeds.

It really had _____ seeds.

# Glasses

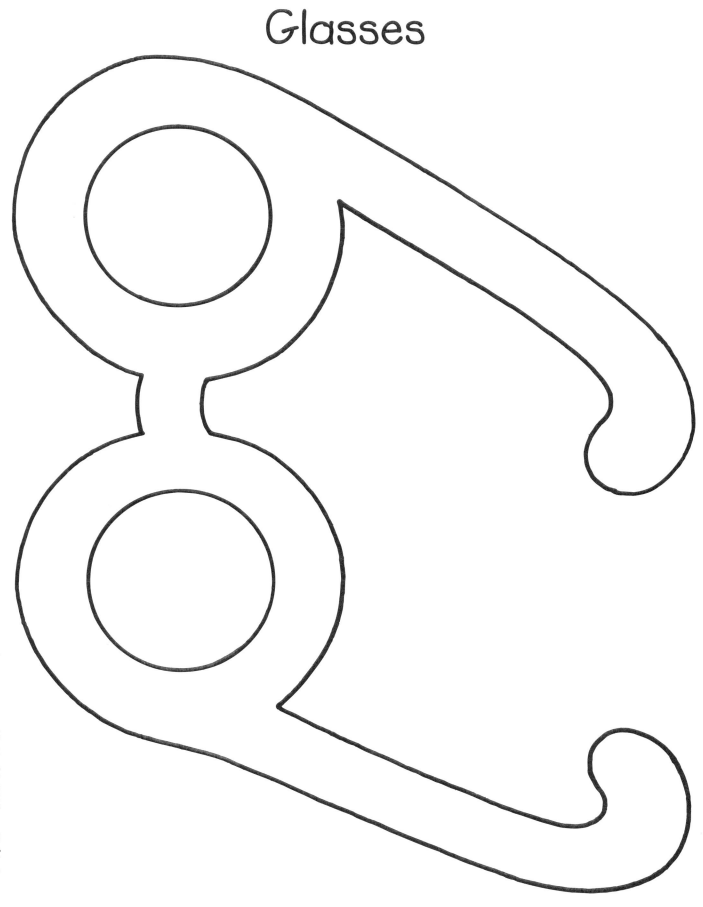

# Beach Bucket

*Making Memories Month by Month* © 2001 Creative Teaching Press

# My Dad

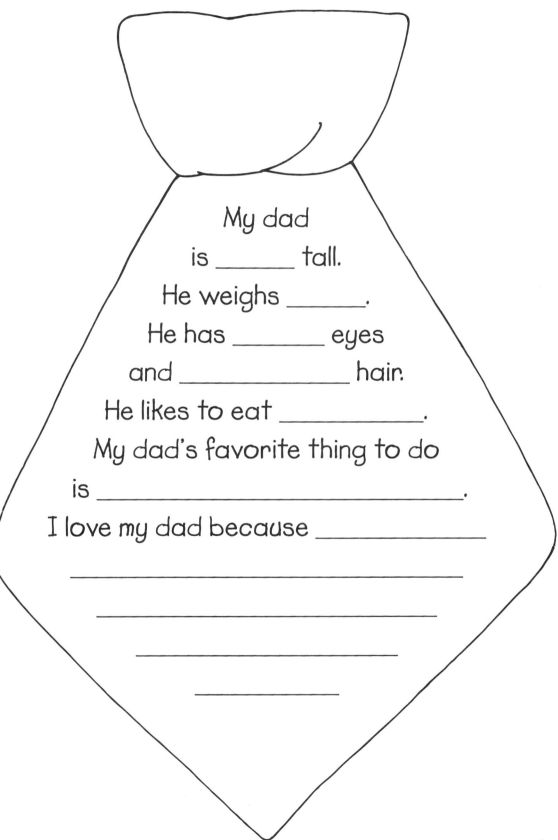

My dad
is _____ tall.
He weighs _____.
He has _____ eyes
and _____ hair.
He likes to eat _____.
My dad's favorite thing to do
is _____.
I love my dad because _____
_____
_____
_____
_____

## June
(to the tune of "Are You Sleeping?")

It is June.
It is June.
Father's Day.
Father's Day.
Summertime is coming.
Summertime is coming.
School is out.
School is out.

# Fish

Paint stripes across children's hand with yellow, purple, green, and red paint. Have children make a sideways handprint on a piece of blue paper. Invite children to use additional paint to add an eye, a mouth, and a gill to their fish.

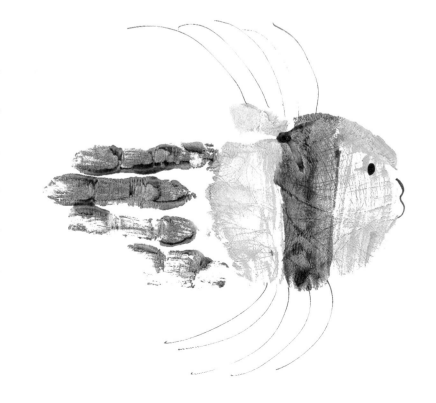

# Something about Me

There's something about me
That I'm knowing.
There's something about me
That's showing . . . I'm growing!

# School Is Out

(to the tune of "Twinkle, Twinkle, Little Star")

It is June and summer's here.
It's the end of this school year.
Boys and girls made new friends.
Teachers lent a helping hand.
We learned a lot and had much fun.
School is out for everyone!

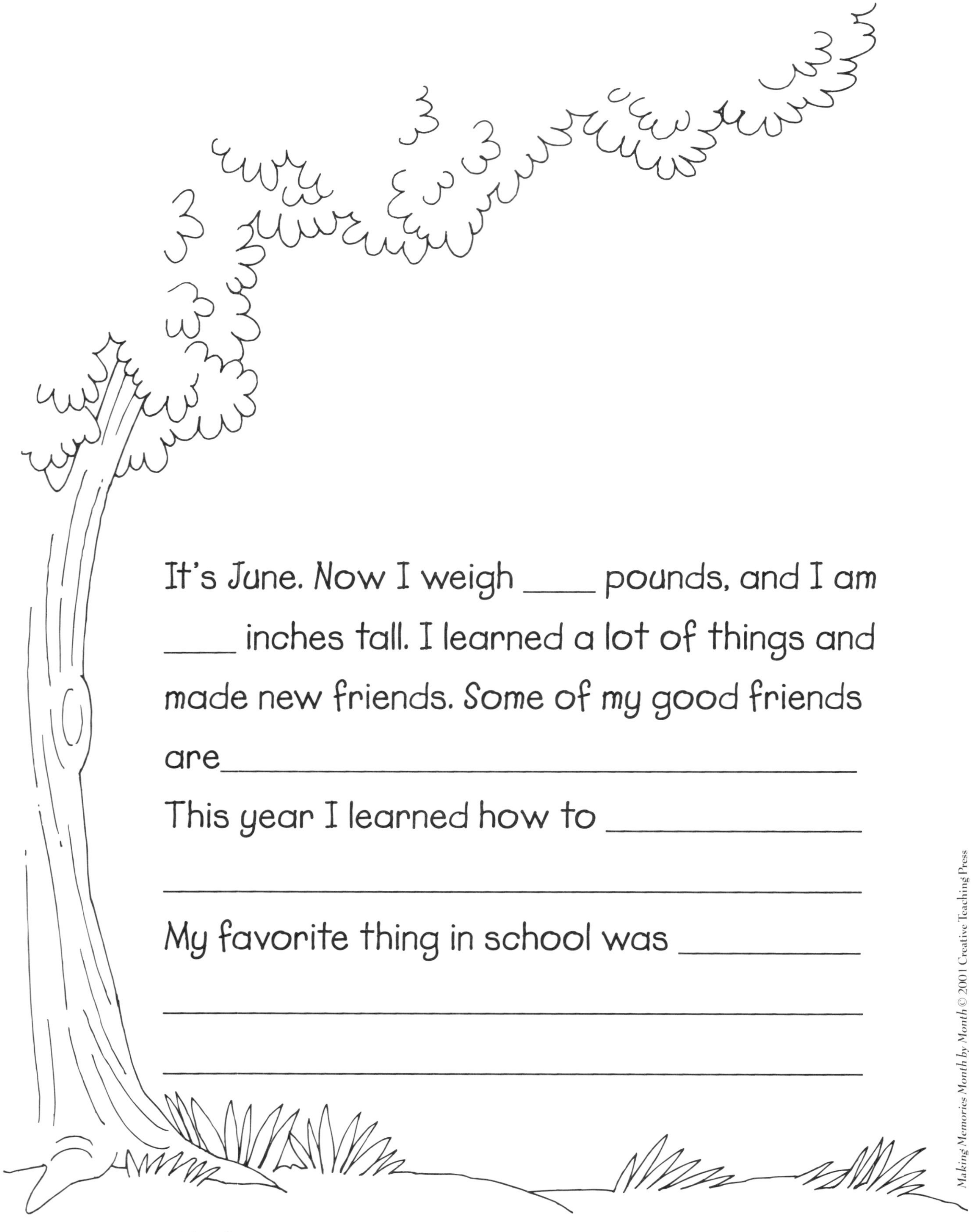

It's June. Now I weigh ____ pounds, and I am ____ inches tall. I learned a lot of things and made new friends. Some of my good friends are_____

This year I learned how to _____

_____

My favorite thing in school was _____

_____

_____

Making Memories Month by Month © 2001 Creative Teaching Press

Making Memories Month by Month © 2001 Creative Teaching Press

# July/August

It's summertime and the weather is warm. What a perfect time to teach a unit on ice cream, camping, or picnics. Or, present a unit on families and have children create a family tree. Don't forget about Independence Day. Children can sing patriotic songs and learn about American history. There is a lot to do during these summer months.

This is how I look in July. It is summer. I like to go to the beach.

This is how I look in August. The weather is warm. I try to keep myself cool by going swimming.

Mrs. Smith took us on a field trip to a pool.

## Literature Links

☆ *All Kinds of Families* by Norma Simon (Albert Whitman)

☆ *Amelia Bedelia's Family Album* by Peggy Parish (Greenwillow Books)

☆ *The Bears' Picnic* by Stan and Jan Berenstain (Random House)

☆ *Curious George Goes to an Ice Cream Shop* by Margret Rey (Houghton Mifflin)

☆ *Fireworks, Picnics, and Flags* by James Cross Giblin (Houghton Mifflin)

☆ *Hurray for the Fourth of July* by Wendy Watson (Clarion Books)

## Family Tree

### Materials

❏ Who Is in My Family? reproducible (page 128)

❏ scissors

❏ sponges

❏ brown, green and red paint/paintbrushes

❏ paper

❏ black marker

Cut sponges into 1¹/₂" (3.8 cm) squares. Have each child take home a Who Is in My Family? reproducible. Have parents complete the form for children to return to school the following day. Invite each child to paint a trunk of a tree on a piece of paper. Then, have children use green paint to sponge-paint the leaves of the tree. Allow the paint to dry, and then invite children to place their finger in red paint and dab it on the tree to make apples. Have children make one apple for each family member. Use a black marker to write a family member's name across each apple. (Refer to each student's completed reproducible for the names.)

## Fireworks Picture

### Materials

❏ "On Independence Day" song (page 130)

❏ red, white, and blue paint

❏ 3 bowls

❏ tape

❏ 9" x 12" (23 cm x 30.5 cm) black construction paper

❏ 13" x 9" x 2" (33 cm x 23 cm x 5 cm) baking pan

❏ marbles

❏ silver glitter

❏ glue

Place red, white, and blue paint in three separate bowls. Tape a piece of black construction paper to the inside of a baking pan. Invite children to take turns placing a marble in the red paint and then in the pan. Encourage children to hold the sides of the pan and tilt it so that the marble rolls all over the paper. Then, have children repeat the procedure with the blue and white paint. Sprinkle some silver glitter over the picture before the paint completely dries. Give each child a copy of the song. Ask children to glue the song to the center of their painting. Have the class sing the song.

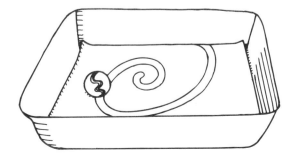

## Ice Cream

## Materials

❏ *Curious George Goes to an Ice Cream Shop* by Margret Rey

❏ July/August frame (page 135)

❏ ingredients and supplies for making ice cream (see recipe)

❏ camera/film

Read aloud *Curious George Goes to an Ice Cream Shop*. After discussing the book, talk about the different flavors of ice cream, and ask children how they think ice cream is made. Have each child use the recipe below to make ice cream. Then, invite children to taste their ice cream. Take photos of the children making and eating the ice cream. Have them write about the experience on a July/August frame. Place the photos and frames in the scrapbooks.

### Ice Cream

Ingredients
- ½ cup milk
- 1 tablespoon sugar
- ¾ tablespoon vanilla
- ice
- 6 tablespoons salt

1. Put the milk, sugar, and vanilla in a small resealable plastic bag, and seal the bag.
2. Fill a large freezer bag half full of ice.
3. Add the salt to the ice.
4. Put the small bag inside the large bag, and seal the large bag.
5. Shake the bag for 5 minutes.
6. Put the bag in a freezer for a few minutes. The liquid will thicken like ice cream.

## Picnic

## Materials

❏ *The Bears' Picnic* by Stan and Jan Berenstain

❏ small paper plates

❏ scissors

❏ old food magazines

❏ crayons or markers/ drawing paper

❏ glue

❏ construction paper

Read aloud *The Bears' Picnic*. Discuss with the class the food that the bears ate. Give each child a small paper plate. Have children cut out from a magazine or draw a picture of a food or picnic item that begins with the first letter of their name. For example, Beth could cut out a picture of beans. Ask children to glue their picture on their plate and then glue their plate to a piece of construction paper. Have children label the paper with their name and the food item (e.g., *Beth's beans*).

# Who Is in My Family?

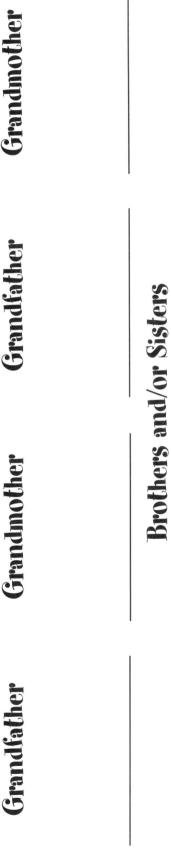

Me

Dad

Mom

Grandfather

Grandmother

Grandmother

Brothers and/or Sisters

Grandfather

## July—Crab

Paint the inside of children's hands with blue paint. Have children press their hands on a piece of white paper so that the heels of each palm are slightly overlapped. Invite children to use a black marker to draw two eyes. Ask children to use orange paint to make claws on each thumbprint.

## August— Caterpillar

Use two colors of tempera paint. Have children dip their thumb into one color of paint and press their thumb on a piece of white paper four times. Tell children to leave a space between each thumbprint. Invite children to choose a different color of paint to make thumbprints with their other thumb. Have them make four prints with the second color. When the paint is dry, invite children to use a black marker to make a face and antennae to complete their caterpillar.

*Making Memories Month by Month* © 2001 Creative Teaching Press

## On Independence Day
(to the tune of "Mary Had a Little Lamb")

We're going to see fireworks, fireworks, fireworks.
We're going to see fireworks
On Independence Day.

We'll celebrate our freedom, freedom, freedom.
We'll celebrate our freedom
On Independence Day.

July 4th is a special day, special day, special day.
July 4th is a special day.
It's Independence Day!

## To Summer

Here's to summer,
Here's to summer,
For the bird,
And the bee,
And the butterfly;
For bright
Sunrays that
Blaze in the sky,
Oh, here's to summer.

Making Memories Month by Month © 2001 Creative Teaching Press

This is how I look in July. It is summer. I like to

_____

_____

_____

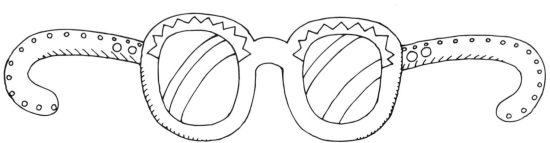

This is how I look in August. The weather is warm. I try to keep myself cool by_____

_____

_____

_____

134   August Writing Paper

Making Memories Month by Month © 2001 Creative Teaching Press

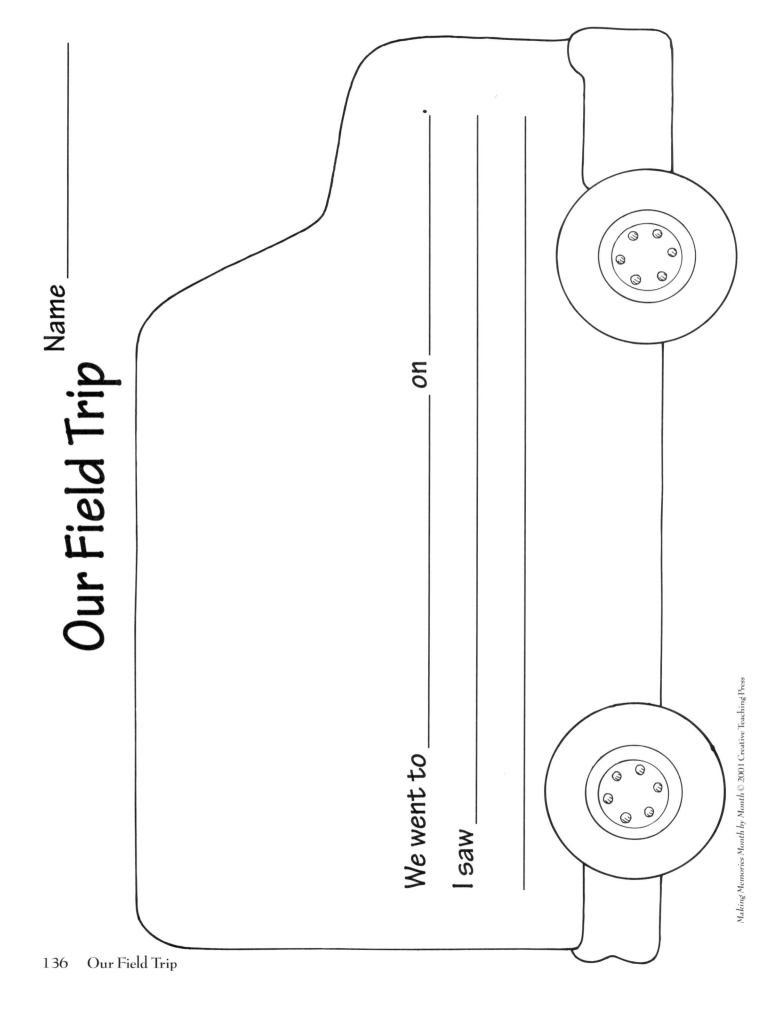

Name

# Our Field Trip

We went to

on

I saw

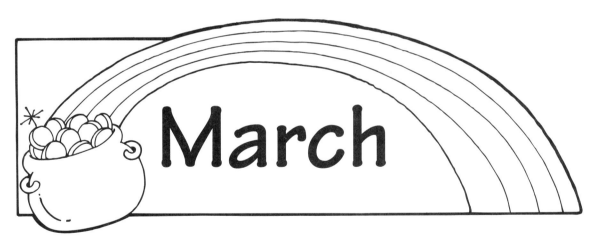

*Making Memories Month by Month* © 2001 Creative Teaching Press

# September

# October

# November

# December

# Autographs

# Fun!

# My Friends

# Wow!

# Look at how much I learned!

# I love school!

# I can write

# Favorites

# What an artist!

# What a year!

*Making Memories Month by Month* © 2001 Creative Teaching Press

## Everyone Has Gifts

Gifts come in many packages.
Gifts are obvious and subtle.
Gifts radiate in a smile.
Gifts shine through compassion.
Gifts resonate in talent.
Gifts are glorified in simple and grand
accomplishments.
Gifts are nurtured in patience and
persistence.
Everyone had unique gifts . . .
Each opened and celebrated on
different occasions.

Author unknown

Thank you for sharing your
most precious gift of all . . .
your child!

---

# Thank you

Dear Parents,

It has been a pleasure working with your child and being a part of an incredible learning journey this year. Your child has grown by leaps and bounds and is on the road to independence. Every child makes this journey in his or her own way. Remember to always treasure your child's special qualities. I hope you enjoy this memory book; it was assembled with much affection. It has been a wonderful year!

Sincerely,

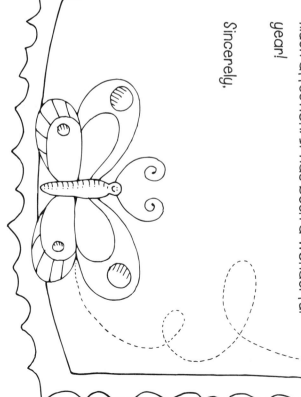

# All About Me

My name is_____. I am _____ years old.

I weigh ____ pounds, and I am _____ inches tall.

I was born on _____ in _____.
DATE                      CITY

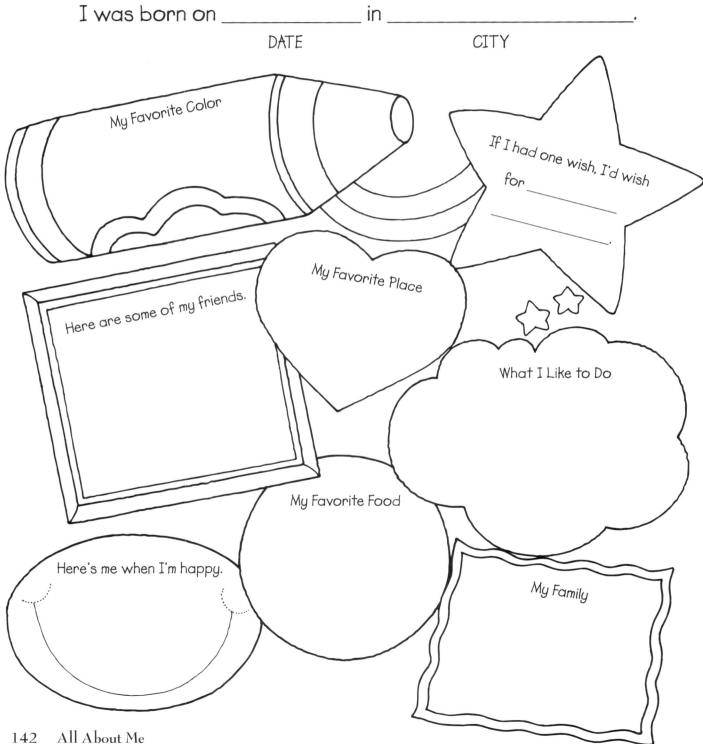

My Favorite Color

If I had one wish, I'd wish for _____ _____.

My Favorite Place

Here are some of my friends.

What I Like to Do

My Favorite Food

Here's me when I'm happy.

My Family

Making Memories Month by Month © 2001 Creative Teaching Press

Making Memories Month by Month © 2001 Creative Teaching Press